WHILE WE WAIT

WHILE WE WAIT

LIVING THE QUESTIONS
OF ADVENT

MARY LOU REDDING

UPPER
ROOM BOOKS®
NASHVILLE

While We Wait
Living the Questions of Advent
Copyright © 2002 by Mary Lou Redding
All rights reserved.

The Upper Room® Web site: http://www.upperroom.org.

Cover art: Natalie Cox Mead
Cover and interior design: Ed Maksimowicz
Interior implementation: PerfecType
Fourth printing: 2007

Library of Congress Cataloging-in-Publication Data

Redding, Mary Lou, 1950-
        While we wait : living the questions of Advent / by Mary Lou Redding.
            p. cm.
        ISBN 978-0-8358-0982-5

1. Advent.   I. Title.
    BV40 .R43 2002
    242'.332—dc21   2002002490

Printed in the United States of America

For
Elizabeth, Joan, and Velma

———————

three wise women with whom I share my journey

CONTENTS

INTRODUCTION
THE QUESTIONS OF ADVENT

Advent is about preparing ourselves to give attention to God's great gift, Jesus Christ. Sometimes we have difficulty believing we will see anything new. After all, we know the story. We've heard it year after year. What could we possibly see or hear that we have not seen and heard before? This book approaches the story from some perspectives that you may not have considered. This book looks at the questions of people in the Christmas stories and at some Bible passages that you may not have explored at this time of year. And as always when we come to scripture, God will speak if we allow ourselves to hear.

The traditional Christmas story that we present and experience in pageants, carols, and worship is actually a composite drawn primarily from three of books of the New Testament—Luke, John, and Matthew. The Gospel of Luke gives us many touching and dramatic "people stories." In Luke we read about the prodigal and his elder brother, the healing of Jairus's daughter, the story of Mary and Martha, the parable of the good Samaritan, the woman searching for her lost coin. Luke also gives us the people stories of Christmas: the shepherds frightened by the appearance of the angels, Gabriel's announcement to Mary that she will bear God's Son, Mary's journey to stay with her cousin Elizabeth, Mary and Joseph bringing Jesus to the temple for circumcision and offering the poor worshipers' sacrifice of two doves. The Gospel of John, always looking for deeper meanings in ordinary things, gives us a theological perspective on the Christmas story in its essay on the Incarnation (John 1:1-18). The Latin word *carne* means "flesh"; to be "incarnate" is to be "in flesh." John speaks beautifully of how God became flesh and came to dwell with mortals (God "moved in with us," according to the *Cotton Patch Version*).

Matthew contributes a different view of the story because Matthew's purpose is different. Matthew does not set out to tell us about the individuals in the drama but to show us how the Christmas events fit into a much larger picture. Matthew writes to show how Jesus' coming fulfills Old Testament prophecies about the Messiah who would deliver God's people. (This Gospel quotes more from Hebrew scripture than any other book in the New Testament.) Matthew also gives us the story of the unnamed Magi coming from "the East"—another country envisioned as a seat of religious wisdom and prophecy—to acknowledge Christ. The account of the Magi's visit demonstrates God's movement beyond the Jewish nation and draws the larger world into the scope of the story.

Matthew's account does not begin with the events and circumstances of Jesus' birth. Matthew delves into history, listing Jesus' genealogy for us. This Gospel aims to show that the child Jesus is the fulfillment of something God has been about for many generations—for thousands of years, in fact. Matthew's genealogy begins the way we'd expect a biblical genealogy to begin—with "begats." But curiously, among the men in Jesus' lineage Matthew also includes the names of three women: Tamar, Rahab, and Ruth. *While We Wait* begins its look at the themes of Advent by examining these three women and the questions they and their lives raise. The book also explores Zechariah's question, then the questions posed by Mary and by Elizabeth, and finally the question asked by the Magi. The last chapter, meant for use after Christmas in the first week of the new year, moves to Epiphany. These people and the questions they ask offer a way to focus our prayer and reflection during the seasons of Advent and Christmastide. Each of these honest searchers offers us instruction and models faithfulness in the midst of their questions.

Though designed for use in small groups, *While We Wait* may also be easily used by individuals. A guide for small-group meetings for each of the four weeks of Advent and for Epiphany week is included as the last chapter of the book. The group sessions are meant to be completed in forty-five minutes. Leadership may rotate among members of the group. Each week's chapter also includes material for individual use between the meetings. Resources for the individual include three components: Reading, Reflection/Journaling Questions, and suggestions for Breath Prayers.

Readings: Participants read a chapter each week, before the group meets. Each chapter focuses on a question asked by one of the people named above. These readings are short and usually can be read in fifteen minutes or less. If you begin the week by reading the chapter, that content can frame daily reflection times over the following days.

Reflection/Journaling Questions: At the end of each chapter, you will find suggested daily Bible readings for five days with reflection/journaling questions that build on these Bible passages. Space is provided in the book for you to record your thoughts. Daily reading and reflection enrich our attending to God during Advent. If you have never written in a journal about your spiritual questions and insights, please consider giving yourself the gift of quiet minutes to do so during this Advent. The small amount of time it takes can be a gift to ourselves and to God as we record our insights and explore what God may be saying to us. If you want to write in a more private place than here in the book, use a blank book or spiral notebook or write at your computer and save your journal on a disk. Begin this reflection time with thirty to sixty seconds of silence to quiet yourself, to become mindful of God's presence. End your silence by asking God to open your mind and heart to what the scripture may say to you.

Breath Prayers: Each reflection also suggests a "breath prayer" to use until the next reflection time. These modern breath prayers are adaptations of an ancient Christian prayer known as the "Jesus Prayer." That prayer is very short: "Lord Jesus Christ, Son of God, have mercy on me, a sinner." Early Christians prayed this prayer continually, fitting it to the rhythm of their breathing. That practice, of course, is the origin of its being called the breath prayer. The address, "Lord Jesus Christ, Son of God," is said inwardly while inhaling. This act symbolizes taking in God and what God wants for us. The petition "Have mercy on me, a sinner" is prayed inwardly while exhaling. That second phrase symbolizes releasing sin (and everything within that is not pleasing to God). The breath prayer was a way of praying "without ceasing," as 1 Thessalonians 5:17 directs. Sometimes people shorten the parts of the prayer to "Lord Jesus Christ" or "Lord Jesus" and "have mercy on me," or even to "Jesus" (inhaling) and "mercy" (exhaling). This extremely shortened form of the prayer is the source of its designation as the Jesus Prayer. The breath prayers suggested in this book are just that: suggestions. You may want to compose your own breath prayers to pray during Advent and Christmastide. Six to eight syllables work best. One part of the prayer is a name for God that is meaningful to you; the other part is a short petition such as "Give me joy" or "Teach me to love." Do whatever seems to fit best with your way of praying.

Being part of a special group during Advent presents an opportunity to come to God in gratitude for God's coming to us. So I invite you to join me and these questioners. Even if you have not used disciplines such as writing or praying a breath prayer before, allow yourself to experiment with them this year. There is no magic in the disciplines, but they are a way to consciously place yourself in God's presence. What are the questions you bring to God? Are yours some of the same ones asked by these folks in the Bible? This study offers a chance to explore your questions and theirs in company with other believers. May each of you hear what God says to you and, through these stories, to all of us.

CHAPTER 1

LIVING IN HOPE: WHAT WILL YOU GIVE ME?

"Hope" is the thing with feathers—

That perches in the soul—

And sings the tune without

the words—

And never stops—at all—

—Emily Dickinson

My young friend Macey came to her parents upset one Christmas after all the gifts had been opened. She had carefully written a Christmas list weeks earlier, and she was dismayed to find that a particular doll she had put on that list was not among her presents. Her parents explained that a Christmas list is suggestions, not demands, but Macey was puzzled. Finally she lamented in frustration, "But I asked Santa for it!"

Macey approached Christmas with expectations that included specific personal benefits, and if we are truthful, most of us probably would have to admit we are sometimes like her. Clearly we have wants. In fact, enterprising garment manufacturers capitalize on this nearly universal expectation by creating holiday sweaters, T-shirts, and sweatshirts bearing various messages to Santa: "Dear Santa, I want it all!" "Dear Santa, I can explain!" "Dear Santa, I've been very, very good." When someone asks, "What do you want for Christmas?" most of us have a ready answer. We can name our wants—what we hope to receive.

The theme often associated with this first week of Advent is hope—our hopes and God's hopes for us and for the world. But the hope of Advent is not like the hope we associate with Christmas gifts or lists. We often use the word *hope* as if hope were a fragile thing. We say, "I hope you can come with us." And someone answers, "I hope so too, but it doesn't look promising."

Hope in such contexts is little more than a wish. It is a vague, anemic desire with no teeth in it and little chance of becoming a reality. The hope we read about in the Bible is much more robust. The people of the Bible reveal a hope worth risking for, hope that pulls people from the present into the future. This hope spills out from one person's life into the lives of others and changes everything. Biblical hope is a powerful force for change.

We're going to view the hope of Advent by looking first at two of the women mentioned by Matthew in Jesus' lineage. You may not have heard much about these women in Sunday school, and their stories read more like plots for a daytime soap opera than what we think of as Bible stories. Their stories are not your typical sweet Christmas tales, and you'd probably have to do some substantial adapting to tell them to the kids at bedtime. The two women are Tamar and Rahab.

TAMAR: HOPE AND COURAGE

Tamar is the earliest of Jesus' foremothers mentioned by Matthew, and she voices the question that guides the reflections in this chapter. She is married to one of the sons of Judah. Judah is one of Jacob's twelve sons and patriarch of one of the twelve tribes of Israel. Tamar asks Judah, "What will you give me?" According to the story in Genesis 38, Tamar is married to Judah's oldest son, Er, who has two brothers, Onan and Shelah. When Er dies because he is "wicked in the sight of the LORD," Shelah is still a boy. Judah tells his middle son, Onan, to fulfill his obligation under the law and marry Tamar. The Jewish law of levirate marriage requires that when a man dies without children, his brother must marry the widow and "give her children." The first son born to the new union becomes heir to the dead brother's property. (This marriage tradition is reflected in the New Testament story of the man who attempts to entrap Jesus with a question about a woman who marries seven brothers in turn, only to have each one die. The man asks Jesus, "In the resurrection whose wife will she be?" [Mark 12:23]).

For some reason not mentioned in the biblical account, Onan does not want to "raise up children to his brother's name." He breaks the law and shirks his obligation to Tamar, doing what he can to be sure that he does not impregnate her. Because of his refusal to meet this obligation, the story tells us, Onan too dies. At this point, Judah sends Tamar back to her father's household to live as a widow. He tells her that when his son Shelah is old enough, Shelah will become Tamar's husband. Because widows who did not have children were essentially helpless under the law, Tamar has no choice but to obey. Since women could not inherit property, Tamar cannot have control of what belonged to her husband Er. Neither can she marry anyone else as long as her husband has brothers or other near male relatives who could marry her. She has no choice and no status.

Tamar goes back to her father's house to wait. She watches her father-in-law, and she watches Shelah grow up. Yet, as Genesis 38:14 tells us, Tamar is not "given to him in marriage." The Bible doesn't tell us how long she waits, but Judah's wife dies and Judah completes the traditional period of mourning. Judah does nothing to bring Tamar back into the household. Tamar waits and waits, with no word from Judah. Finally Tamar decides to take action. She comes up with a daring plan, one that could cost her life. But for a woman of her time, to be childless is almost as bad as death. In the generation before Tamar, Rachel cried out to Jacob in anguish, "Give me children, or I shall die!" (Gen. 30:1). Childlessness equaled no influence on the world, no future.

But Tamar also acts. Somehow she learns that Judah plans to help in a sheep shearing, and she finds out where. Putting off her widow's garments, Tamar disguises herself as a prostitute and waits at the edge of the town where Judah is to visit. When Judah comes by and sees her, he decides to become a customer. Tamar, bargaining, asks him, "What will you give me?" He promises her a sheep but unfortunately doesn't have one with him. She then asks him for a pledge to hold until he comes back with the sheep in payment. He agrees, giving her his signet, cord, and staff as a guarantee that he will pay later. As soon as Judah leaves, Tamar removes her disguise and returns home. Judah later sends a friend with the promised lamb to pay the "prostitute," but she is nowhere to be found. Townspeople say no prostitute has been in the place. Judah and his friend stop asking because "otherwise [they would] be laughed at" (Gen. 38:23) for being fooled by a woman. Being laughed at apparently would be worse than having visited a prostitute, whether or not his period of mourning had ended.

Fast forward three months: Tamar is pregnant. Someone reports to Judah that his daughter-in-law has disgraced his family as an adulteress. (She is in a sense "married" to the family, whether or not she has a living husband, and sexual contact with anyone would be considered adultery.) Obviously pregnancy is proof of sexual contact. Judah says, "Bring her out, and let her be burned," evidently the punishment for having sex outside marriage. But Tamar has kept the objects Judah gave her, and she sends them to him with this message: "It was the owner of these who made me pregnant" (Gen. 38:25). Seeing his own belongings, Judah immediately admits his wrong treatment of Tamar in withholding Shelah and marriage, saying, "She is more in the right than I, since I did not give her to my son Shelah."

It is difficult for us to interpret this rather strange story without understanding that disgrace, insecurity, and low status accompany widowhood for women in Tamar and Judah's culture. To be childless is terrible; to be a widow is a disgrace (Isa. 54:4). When a woman's husband dies, that event may be regarded as punishment for wickedness, either the man's or the woman's. Tamar has no children, and two husbands have died. She is not free to marry anyone else as long as her husband's brother has a claim on her, and so she lives in limbo, waiting to see if Judah will do what decency and the law require. With no children and no husband, she will have no one to care for her as she grows old. It is easy to see how she could become desperate. To secure a permanent place in the family, she needs to marry Judah's remaining son and bear a child.

As for Judah, he does not seem to be a terrible man. He attempts to honor his business agreement with the prostitute, and he readily admits his dishonorable conduct. And as Genesis 38:11 tells us, he simply feared Shelah "would die, like his brothers" if he married Tamar. Judah does not know that wickedness and disobedience were the reasons his first two sons died, and so perhaps he thinks some wickedness on Tamar's part has led to their deaths. He loved these sons, and he loves the remaining one; upholding tradition and observing the law are less important to him than saving Shelah. Most of us can probably understand a parent's feeling that way. He is not a terrible man.

Yet Judah's reluctance to insist that Shelah carry out his responsibility has created for Tamar a life that in their culture is not a life at all. What is she supposed to do? Languish until she is too old to marry and bear children? For me, Tamar is a picture of hope and courage in the face of great loss and vulnerability. I can imagine her lying awake at night, wondering why Judah has not called her back into the family, wondering if she will ever know the joy and status of motherhood. I can also imagine her hatching the plan that is played out in the Genesis story. It may have taken her months of constructing possible scenarios before she came up with a scheme that could work. Even if her plan proceeds smoothly and she succeeds in securing an object of Judah's to serve as her proof of the sexual union, there is still no guarantee that she will conceive a child. Judah might still deny her claim that he was the one who impregnated her. He could say that she stole his belongings. After all, in the story as it is told in Genesis, she has no witnesses. If he denounces her, she could be burned alive as an adulteress. But Tamar trusts that he will not allow her to die. Or maybe, as the song says, "Freedom's just another word for nothing left to lose." Tamar is free to try her bold plan because she has nothing to lose.

In asking Judah, "What will you give me?" Tamar is thoroughly human and honest—and clever. Her question echoes what we often ask God, figuratively or literally: "How can I know that this will work out, God? What guarantee will you give me?" In the New Testament, we read about a character in the Christmas narrative who asks almost the same question: Zechariah, father of John the Baptist. While serving his turn in the temple, he enters the holy place to burn incense and there an angel appears. The angel tells Zechariah that his prayers have been heard, that he and his wife, Elizabeth, will become parents. Since Zechariah and his wife are both "well stricken in years," he asks, "How will I know that this is so?" Who can blame Zechariah for asking for proof? After all, he is terrified from the time the angel appears. (Some of us might say we'd be convinced of anything by the presence of an angel, but I think I'd probably react as Zechariah does. I'd want something to hold on to once the angel disappeared.) In this case, of course, the eventual birth of the baby, John, will be proof that "this is so." But Zechariah will not be the one who is pregnant, with his body providing evidence. He will have to take his wife's word for months to come. He is asking for a sign—for help to feel sure, for reassurance— but he does not get any. In fact, the angel announces that because of this questioning, Zechariah will be unable to speak until the baby is born. This means not only that Zechariah will be mute but that he will have no way of explaining his experience with the angel and telling Elizabeth that God is about to fulfill their hopes and answer their prayers. Zechariah and Elizabeth have been waiting a long time for a child and probably have suffered many false hopes and disappointments through the years. Zechariah is like many of us in asking for a sign.

BRINGING OUR HOPES TO GOD

Like Tamar, when we come to God with our hopes, we also bring our frustrated hopes. We've all had times when what we hoped for did not come. Our excitement and expectation as we look for good things to come are often mixed with memories of times when plans fell through, when promises were not kept, when people disappointed us. We rarely approach any hope with absolutely no doubt or question, and the same is true when we approach God. When people have failed us or we have failed ourselves, that sense of failure can creep into our hope. Christmas can be, in fact, a time when unfulfilled hopes rise up to haunt us—or to taunt us. Memories of holidays that were less than we wanted them to be generate sadness and dread mixed with the joy we hope for during the Christmas season. Tamar, risking her life and future as she does, must surely feel fear as well as hope. Her question to Judah also implies that she cannot trust him completely. Her request for a guarantee is one we'd probably all like to make of God: "Give me something I can touch and hold on to, God, to let me know that you know about my situation. Give me something to prove that you will do what you say."

God's response is stark: "I guarantee absolutely nothing, yet I will give you everything. All you have to do is give me yourself." Trust is built on experience, and we learn to trust God—we learn that God is working in our life and in the world around us—by taking small risks and seeing God act. We may decide that we will trust God to help us with some relatively small issue in our lives. For example, I may be a person who is terrified of speaking before a group. Someone asks me to teach Sunday school at church, and I agree, with fear and trembling, and start praying that God will help me. As I look toward the first Sunday, the thought of standing before the group is torture. I worry that I won't have anything to say or that what I do say will sound stupid. Or I worry that no one will participate, and the group will sit in stony silence. But I prepare carefully and pray fervently, and the class goes all right. There are some awkward moments, but the time passes. In the following weeks I call on some other teachers for suggestions when I am preparing a particularly difficult lesson, and they are glad to talk it through with me. Week after week, class members return. After a few months, I am able to be more relaxed, and before I know it, six months has passed. The person who recruited me says, "See? I told you God would help you!" I realize that God has been helping me, all along. I did not realize it on those evenings and Saturday afternoons when I was poring over the curriculum, but God was helping me. The help was so unspectacular that I did not notice it, but God was there. Trusting God begins with small issues and moves on to other, larger ones.

In the Book of Malachi God says, "Prove me . . . [and] I will . . . pour you out a blessing" (Mal. 3:10, KJV). That word *prove* means test, as in the phrase "proving ground." In other words, God says, "Go ahead. Test me. Let me show you. . . ." Trust does build on experience, and as we decide to trust God in small situations in our lives, we learn on deeper and deeper levels that God can be trusted. We "test" God, and in the process, we prove to ourselves that God can be trusted.

There are limits to the parallels we can draw between ourselves and the characters in Bible stories, but as I think about Tamar and Judah, I can see that we often approach God tentatively, as Tamar approaches Judah. Tamar probably takes the chance with Judah that she does because of earlier experiences with him. Though we aren't given details in the Book of Genesis, something in her experience allows Tamar to risk. She must believe that Judah is basically a good and honorable man. If not, she could lose her life. Powerless as she is, Tamar finds a way to open the door to what she wants and needs. Somehow, in those weeks and months of waiting, she finds a way to keep her hope alive and eventually to act on it. That is the first part of her story. But that is not the end of her story. When Tamar risks, God allows her to conceive, and when the time comes for Tamar to give birth, she bears not one son but twins. She secures a place for herself in the family, and Judah has not one son but three. Her hope and her risking make a difference not just for her but for Judah, the man whose fear for his one remaining son had limited both their lives. The outgrowth of her hope and courage spill over into his life as well.

RAHAB: HOPE AND OPPORTUNITY

While Tamar merely pretends to be a prostitute, Rahab, the next woman mentioned in Matthew's lineage of Jesus, actually is a prostitute. Rahab lives in a house on the wall that surrounds Jericho (the walls that will "come tumbling down" when Joshua and the Hebrews march around them seven times on the seventh day). Rahab's role in the story of God's people illustrates how important a single individual can be. She is not a person of position or power, but she is a person of courage, vision, and yes, hope. She is courageous enough to defy the king's soldiers, and she has a vision of a better future. When Rahab has a chance, she bargains not just for herself but for her family. She is really quite a woman. When an opportunity presents itself, she seizes the moment. Her story is told in the Book of Joshua.

The Israelites, led by Joshua, are readying a military campaign against the city of Jericho. In preparation, Joshua sends spies into the city. As in an old western movie, they find a good-hearted prostitute, Rahab, who provides them a place to hide. When the king's soldiers hear that spies are inside the walls, they mount what seems to be a house-to-house search and show up at Rahab's door. She boldly faces them down, lies to the soldiers to throw them off the trail ("They went thataway"?), and tells the spies how to evade the searchers. (Perhaps she had been involved in something like this before.) In exchange for her assistance, she exacts a promise from these spies: When the conquering army sacks the city, she and her family will be spared. They give her a scarlet cord, the secret sign to be displayed in her window to guarantee her household's safety when the Israelites return. She is not a sterling character, but she is certainly a strong one.

What Is Hope?

What do Tamar and Rahab have to tell us about hope? First of all, they show us that hope faces reality. Hope is not merely putting on a happy face, denying our needs and frustrations, and mouthing familiar phrases about how good God is. Hope faces squarely what life is and what it is not. Tamar faces the fact that Judah has not brought his son Shelah forward to marry her. She could make excuses to herself and others (and perhaps she does that for a while) about her situation. She could meekly accept her fate. She could keep herself busy with nieces and nephews and push aside her own desire to have a child. But she doesn't do that. She pays attention to her father-in-law's lack of attention to her, and she decides to take action. She risks her life for the chance of something better.

Rahab takes a similar approach. She does not pretend that hiding Hebrew spies is an innocent exercise. Neither does she pretend that her nation is going to defeat Joshua and the Israelite army. She admits her fear and the fear of her people, saying that their hearts "melted" because of it. Rahab coolly assesses the situation and decides to cast her lot with God. In fact, Rahab voices clearly the truth that is the basis for our hope as well as for hers. She says to the Hebrews, "The LORD your God is indeed God in heaven above and earth below" (Josh. 2:11). That is, the God of heaven, Creator of the universe, is more than a remote God out there in the sky somewhere. The God she proclaims is God also on earth, a God who is concerned with our daily lives, with all that concerns us. And like Tamar, Rahab makes a leap of faith. She decides to hide the Hebrew spies and to lie to the king's henchmen who come to her door. If her lie is discovered—if the spies are discovered hidden in the stalks of flax on her roof—she no doubt will be killed. But as the song quoted earlier says, Rahab too has nothing left to lose. Joshua and his army are going to sack the city, its inhabitants executed. Rahab is realistic enough to see what is about to happen. Jericho is going to fall, and facing the threat of death, she sees a way to life. She acknowledges God's power and involvement in what is going on, and she decides to become a part of it.

Hope also acknowledges a higher reality, a reality beyond what we can see. When Rahab says, "The LORD your God is indeed God in heaven above and earth below," she tells us something very important. What we see is never all that there is; God is here, in what we see and feel, and God is more than that. Rahab believes that, beyond the dangers and difficulties of her life, God has power available for her situation. That belief in God is an important part of scriptural hope.

HOPE THAT ACTS

These two unlikely women, Tamar and Rahab, become a part of Jesus' lineage. Because of their commitment to the hopes in their hearts, they find courage to risk. One of them faces down one man; the other faces an army. It may be difficult for us to see what they do as honorable. They trick people; they lie; both use their sexuality in ways we probably don't approve of. Their methods are not ones we'd endorse or recommend. Yet they are singled out in scripture, and they become part of what God is doing. When I try to understand their actions, I am reminded of the parable of the shrewd manager in Luke 16. The steward who is about to be fired is commended for "adjusting" debtors' accounts to ensure he will have friends once he is dismissed by his employer. The parable ends with a statement about God's people needing to be wise, to be shrewd. God's people are encouraged to be realists who assess what is happening and then act on their hope for something more than the reality they see. Tamar and Rahab certainly act out of that hope. And they become a part of bringing God into the world in a completely new way.

Another truth surfaces in the stories of these women: We do not have to understand the whole of what God is doing in order to be part of it. Neither of these women mentions any interest in or vision of winning a place in Israel's history. They are not bent on being heroes. They are simply living their lives. Tamar wants a family and pursues accomplishing that; Rahab wants safety for herself and those she loves. These are not the earth-shattering hopes of two women out to change the world. As Tamar and Rahab attentively live the lives they have been given, God uses them. What they do becomes a part of what God is doing, part of something that will change the world—in ways they never foresee. These women tell us that in our daily acts of dealing with our own responsibilities, we are part of something beyond our small sphere of influence. Let's face it: Most of us will never be famous. Few of us will ever be applauded by hordes of people in our lifetime. These women are not. But what they are part of, God's influence in the world, has outlasted the deeds of kings and princes who ruled their lands, the famous people of their day.

When I was in school we read a poem about a grave monument commissioned by a king named Ozymandias in his own honor. The monument stands in the middle of a vast desert, surrounded only by sand dunes as far as the eye can see. On its base appears this ironic message to the ages: "My name is Ozymandias, king of kings: Look on my works, ye Mighty, and despair!" All Ozymandias thought he had done has come to nothing more than a few hunks of stone. Without meaning to, Ozymandias tells us that while those who are mighty by human standards may experience a flash of fame, what they do may leave no lasting impression on the world or on us. What they hope will become a monument to their greatness may become lost in the deserts of time and be seen by almost no one. What the world calls greatness may not be lasting greatness at all.

A quiz making its way around cyberspace focuses on this same idea. The questionnaire begins with ten questions about people who have been in the news. Readers are asked to list facts like the teams that competed in the Super Bowl two years ago, the names of any two Heisman Trophy winners over the last ten years, the author of any novel on the best-seller list, the winners of the Oscar for best actor and actress last year, the names of the four major-party candidates in the presidential race three elections ago, and so on. A second set of ten questions follows. These ask readers to name a teacher who made a difference in their life, someone who showed them an act of kindness during a difficult time, a relative who has made them feel special, a neighbor who taught something important, a friend who has been constant in their life over the years, and so on. Doing the quiz makes it clear that people who may never see their names in a newspaper headline or hear them on the evening news affect us more significantly than the "big" names. Ordinary people shape us, and through all of us, the world. The acts of ordinary people are important.

Tamar and Rahab are not frail, delicate flowers of genteel womanhood. Their hope is not dressed in lace and organza, thin and vulnerable. It is hope in blue jeans, hope that gets its hands dirty. These women's lives present a picture of people working alongside a God whose hands already show the marks of involvement in our lives. They illustrate hope that confronts, that honestly names needs and dreams, hope that is willing to risk, to take whatever action it can, and to trust God to do the rest. In this Advent season, Tamar and Rahab invite us to consider that God is at work as we work, that God is using and will use our lives to bring new life into the world. In this Advent season, they invite us to name before God our dearest hopes—the dreams we hold in our hearts—and to welcome God into those hopes and dreams.

THE NEED FOR HOPE

The world needs people of hope. I think of a friend of my family's, a man who was a part of my life from the time I was a child. I'll call him Virgil. Virgil was a dreamer and a small-time inventor. He had a way with anything mechanical. Motors and engines fascinated him, and he was the best mechanic and sick-car diagnostician I have ever known. Once while I was traveling with a friend and my child, my car began acting up. It was late at night, and I pulled into a service station that posted a sign saying, "Mechanic on duty." (Yes, this was some years ago. Who has mechanics at night these days? Or during the day, for that matter?) The two young men working there were clueless about what might be wrong with my car. I needed to get on my way, but I was reluctant to set out, only to have the car stop for good on the highway. What to do? Then I thought of Virgil. I called him on the pay phone. Sleepily, he answered the phone. I related my situation, and he asked of the car, "What's it doing?" I gave him a careful description of the problem, and he said, "Well, it sounds like it's probably the starter, and there's a way to find out. Take a screwdriver and. . . ." I did what he instructed, and soon we were on our way.

Virgil operated a car-repair business for most of the years of his adult life, but that was not what energized him. Inventing energized him. Constantly working on some new thing that he expected would make him a millionaire, he wanted to leave his family a legacy of his fame and fortune. Over the years he patented a few things, but Virgil never succeeded with his car business or with his inventions. At the time of his death he was still working on one of his dreams (or "schemes," to some in his family). Virgil's family didn't understand his passion, and over the years I heard many heated discussions about the money and time he was wasting on "that silliness" of inventing. I didn't see it or him that way. I saw him as the kind of person this world needs. We need dreamers who waste time on the "silliness" of a passion that pulls them into the future. We need people like Virgil and Tamar and Rahab to shake us loose from our mundane routine, to challenge our tendency to think that what we see is all there is. We need dreamers, people willing to invest their energy in what they hope for.

The questions that Tamar asks Judah, "What will you give me?" and that Zechariah asks the angel, "How will I know . . . ?" remind us that hope does not build on certainty.

To hope means we cannot be completely sure. There are no guarantees. Coming to God with a mixture of hope and excitement is normal and human. We may even experience less welcome feelings alongside hope, such as anxiety, fear, and distrust. But those feelings are acceptable. God welcomes us with whatever degree and quality of hope possible for us. Even if the hope is simply an inexpressible desire for something more, it has power, and its power grows as we nurture the hope in God's presence. The psalmist says, "You, O LORD, are my hope, / my trust, O LORD, from my youth" (Ps. 71:5). When we anchor our hope in God's steady love and good plans for us, hope becomes a permanent part of us. We have hope not because we are powerful or smart or resourceful but because of who God is. And as we test our hope by acting on it, we release God's power into our circumstances. Our "hope muscle" grows stronger and our desire for God more compelling, just as exercising strengthens our physical muscles. As we consciously work with God, we will see more evidence of God's work in the world around us. The more we hope and watch, the more we will see that reinforces our hope and trust.

A dog friend of mine, a golden retriever named Luther, has given me an image of hope that always makes me smile—and think. Luther is a very large dog, well over one hundred pounds. He walks his owner every day in a park-like area near my home. Retrievers are hunting dogs, of course, and Luther enthusiastically embodies his heritage. He hunts moles, chipmunks, and squirrels with great joy, occasionally catching one if he lunges when his human is not expecting Luther's powerful tug on the leash. One autumn morning, Luther and his owner were walking near a stand of trees that is home to many squirrels. On this particular morning, something wonderful, rare, and totally unexpected happened: A squirrel fell out of a tree, right in front of Luther. He had only to pounce. He was astounded—and overjoyed. From that moment on, Luther has believed that squirrels fall out of trees. The next morning, and for many mornings after, Luther approached that stand of trees with his eyes lifted, aquiver with anticipation. He would stop every few feet and look up in eager attention, waiting for a squirrel to fall in front of him.

What if you and I walked through life with that kind of expectation, waiting for God to show up in the midst of our daily activities, for gifts of grace and healing to fall into our lives so close that we can reach out and touch them? What would be different if we lived that way? Living in hope and expectation does not mean that we do nothing. Tamar and Rahab show us that. And Luther has not given up chasing squirrels. He no longer stops every day to wait under those trees; he expends his energy. But he also still pauses from time to time to gaze longingly at the branches overhead. Who knows? It could happen again. And when it does, Luther will be ready, because he knows that sometimes squirrels do fall out of trees. He knows and appreciates with all the energy of his nature that wonderful, unexpected, and totally undeserved gifts can come into our lives.

Wonderful things happen. Most of the time, they come after we've done a lot of work; but sometimes, like Luther's squirrel or like the coming of the baby at Christmas, they are pure gift. Those of us who are looking may even see these wonders in the making. In this season of hope, we are invited to look for the wonders that show us God is still at work in our world and in us. "What will you give me?" we ask. Hope holds with it the promise that God always answers our question by showing up, not necessarily with what we ask for but with remarkable gifts that change our lives and the world.

REFLECTION PAGES

DAY 1 REFLECTION

Read Genesis 38.

Reflect.

Try to imagine yourself in Tamar's situation. When have you felt powerless in a situation that affected you day after day? Were you able to remain hopeful? What or who helped you to be hopeful?

_____

_____

_____

_____

_____

_____

What do you suppose Tamar was feeling as she waited for Judah's reply after sending him his signet and other belongings? In what ways can you identify with her situation of awaiting a response or reaction? Are you waiting for something important as Christmas approaches?

_____

_____

_____

_____

_____

_____

_____

Consider Judah's fear for his son's life versus the demands of the law regarding Tamar. When have you felt pulled between what your heart wanted to do and what "the rules" dictated as the right thing to do in a situation?

_____

_____

_____

_____

If you ever feel pulled between obligations within your family at holiday times, how do you resolve competing interests? How do you feel during these times? What would you like to be able to do?

_____

_____

_____

_____

_____

_____

Rest.

Sit quietly in God's presence and hold in the light of God's love any concerns that have come to mind as you worked through these reflection questions.

Pray a breath prayer.

For the next twenty-four hours, whenever you find yourself waiting (for a phone to be answered, for a computer to come on, for a traffic light to change), pray this prayer with the rhythm of your breathing: "O God, you are my hope." In your mind, say, "O God," as you inhale and "you are my hope" as you exhale.

DAY 2 REFLECTION

Read Joshua 2:1-21.

Reflect.

What positive traits do you see in Rahab? Can you think of ways you would like to be more like her?

_____

_____

_____

When you consider that God worked through a prostitute, how do you react? Is God likely to use some people rather than others? If so, what types of people do you think those would be?

_____
_____
_____
_____
_____
_____
_____

Which people in your life would you not expect God to use or speak through? When have you seen or heard about God's using an unlikely person?

_____
_____
_____
_____
_____
_____
_____

Think about your attitude toward yourself in relation to God. Would you expect God to use you or not to use you? Why?

_____
_____
_____
_____
_____
_____

Rahab stated what she believed about God. What are two or three of your core beliefs about God?

_____
_____
_____
_____
_____

Rest.

Sit quietly and hold in the light of divine love the people God uses to help and guide you.

Pray a breath prayer.

For the next twenty-four hours, pray a breath prayer, such as, "God of surprises, let me see you," or, "God of love, use me for good."

DAY 3 REFLECTION

Read Isaiah 54.

Reflect.

This passage describes the grief of one who has been abandoned or cast aside. Do you know people whose mates have left them? those whose mates have died? What does Isaiah say that might help people who feel alone?

When have you felt abandoned by God or thought that God was far away from you? What helped you or helps you during such times?

_____
_____
_____
_____
_____
_____
_____
_____
_____
_____
_____
_____
_____

Imagine that you are writing a letter to Tamar in her widowhood. What verses from this chapter would you avoid quoting to her? What verses would you quote to give her comfort?

What words in this passage from Isaiah give you hope for the future?

_____

_____

_____

_____

_____

_____

_____

_____

_____

_____

Rest.

Sit quietly in God's presence and think about any friends or acquaintances who may be feeling lonely as Christmas approaches. What do you ask God on their behalf?

Pray a breath prayer.

For the next twenty-four hours, at times when your body is busy but your mind is free to turn to God, pray inwardly with the rhythm of your breathing, "God of compassion, love the world through me."

Day 4 Reflection

Read Habakkuk 2:1-3.

Reflect.

Imagine yourself as the guard watching from a tower on the edge of the city. What are you watching for? What image on the horizon would delight you?

_____
_____
_____
_____
_____
_____
_____

Habakkuk urges us to wait and to believe that God will act. What have you been waiting and hoping for, for a long time? What are you doing or could you do to make your hope into reality?

_____
_____
_____
_____
_____
_____
_____

"There is still a vision for the appointed time." How would you describe this "time" in your life? Which of the four seasons—spring, summer, fall, winter—would you say characterizes your life right now? Why?

_____
_____
_____
_____
_____
_____

Think of someone who is waiting for something—expectant parents, a person waiting to hear about a job, someone at the bedside of a terminally ill loved one. Drawing on your own experience with God during times of waiting, what would you say to this person or these people?

_____

_____

_____

_____

_____

_____

_____

_____

Rest.

Sit quietly and name before God the hopes that are in your heart as Christmas approaches this year. Ask God's help in seeing what you are to do as you wait.

Pray a breath prayer.

For your breath prayer over the next twenty-four hours, offer into God's care your hopes and dreams. Use a few words to describe your hopes (health, peace, forgiveness, reconciliation) or simply say, "God of my heart, I give you my hopes."

DAY 5 REFLECTION

Read Matthew 1:1-17.

Reflect.

How many generations of ancestors can you trace back in your family?

_____

_____

What are your feelings about being able to trace your ancestry or not being able to trace it? Do you consider ancestry important? Why or why not?

_____
_____
_____
_____
_____
_____

What positive traits in yourself can you link to your heritage? Who are you like in your family? Whom do you want to be like?

_____
_____
_____
_____
_____
_____

Shifting your thoughts from your bio-logical family to your "faith family," who has taught you about God? Who taught that person or those people? Name the denominational traditions from which your faith has grown.

_____
_____
_____
_____
_____
_____

What difference, if any, does it make to you that Jesus' lineage is traced in the Bible? Why do you think this passage is included in the Gospel of Matthew?

_____
_____
_____
_____
_____

Rest.

Picture in your mind two or three people who have nurtured you, who have taken care of you. Give thanks for their lives and bless them.

Pray a breath prayer.

For the next twenty-four hours, make your breath prayer an expression of gratitude for life. Use this prayer or one of your own making: "Creator God, thank you for life."

CHAPTER 2

FINDING A HOME: WHY HAVE I FOUND FAVOR IN YOUR SIGHT?

"Home is the place where, when you

have to go there,

They have to take you in."

"I should have called it

Something you somehow haven't to

deserve."

—Robert Frost

W hy have I found favor in your sight, . . . a foreigner?" asks Ruth, another of the women in Jesus' lineage. She asks the question in amazement. Her question strikes a chord in me when I consider that God has taken notice of me and accepted me. Do you ever yearn to be completely known and at the same time completely accepted? I think most of us do. Yet we also live with the fear that anyone who really knows us fully—our weaknesses and our shortcomings—could not possibly accept us. No matter how many good traits we have, we tend to give more weight to what we see as our deficiencies. Many influences in our lives, from our parents' and teachers' admonitions ("Now I want you to be good little boys and girls") to athletic and beauty contests, condition us to evaluate ourselves against an ideal of perfection. When we take that measure, we always see our flaws. And since anything less than perfect is unacceptable, we are unacceptable. This way of looking at ourselves can begin very early in life.

Most of us learn our basic stance toward self in the context of our closest relationships, usually in our families. I am no exception. I know that my family affected how I experience the world and how I see myself. I am one of seven children. To be more precise, I am the middle child of seven children, with two brothers and a sister older and two brothers and a sister younger. I am the exact middle of the progression, and long before I read birth-order psychology about the traits of middle children, I knew that I was different from my siblings in many ways. In fact, I often felt as if I had been dropped into the middle of a strange country—"Who are these people, and why am I being forced to live with them?" The fact that I looked nothing like the rest of my family didn't help. My father had a prominent nose in a distinctive face, and a strong family resemblance was evident in the other children. People often commented on the resemblance among my siblings—and on the fact that I with my red hair and green eyes was an anomaly. As far as I ever heard or thought, I didn't look like anyone except me. And, siblings being what they are, mine made sure that they helped me realize how different I was.

I wondered at times if I actually belonged with this group. Maybe I had been switched at birth with some other baby born at the same time (but then I found out I had been born in a small, rural clinic where there were no other babies to switch me with). Maybe I was a foundling. Though I do not remember actually being told by my siblings (as happens in many families) that I was adopted and not really related to them, I do remember thinking that my being adopted would surely explain a lot that puzzled me. I just didn't belong. My brain seemed to work differently than that of anyone else in the family. I liked different music, different activities, and different kinds of people. I even liked vegetables. For my brothers, this last trait was compelling evidence that I was a different sort of creature than they were. I considered that if I hadn't been adopted *by* the family, maybe I could be adopted *from* them. I often fantasized about being whisked away from this family to one more to my liking, one where I would be appreciated for the wonderful creature that I was.

To make matters worse, I was a science-fiction buff. (Can you guess where this is going?) I began to wonder if I might in fact be an alien. Maybe I came not just from another family but from another planet. Could it be? My younger brothers, particularly, encouraged that line of thinking as we watched *Lost in Space* and *Star Trek*. Yes, that would explain it all! I was an alien, so different that I would never fit in. I would never really understand these people, and they would never be able to understand me because we came from different worlds.

Years later when I began analyzing novels and short stories in literature classes, the concept of alienation felt familiar to me. For me, professors didn't have to spend a lot of time explaining what they meant when they spoke of a character dealing with alienation. Feeling disconnected from those around me and from their ways of thinking and behaving, feeling as if I had no place in the world as most people see it—I'd grown up experiencing that. I knew what it was to feel like an alien. I had personal insight into the feeling behind the literary theme. I yearned to feel that I belonged.

So when I read Ruth's question in the Bible, I identified immediately with her wonder at being accepted. When she asked Boaz, "How have I found favor in your sight, . . . a foreigner?" she surely knew about being a stranger, an alien. She and her mother-in-law, Naomi, had come back to Judah as refugees. Ruth was not even an Israelite; she was a Moabitess and had married into Naomi's family.

The Story of Naomi and Ruth

Naomi and her husband, Elimelech, and their two sons, Chilion and Mahlon, leave Bethlehem in a time of famine. They go to Moab in search of food. Elimelech dies, leaving Naomi with her two sons. The sons marry Moabite women. Chilion marries a woman named Orpah, and Mahlon marries Ruth. Then tragedy strikes; both Chilion and Mahlon die. Naomi and her two daughters-in-law are left widows, all of them. As childless widows, they are doubly cursed: first in having lost their husbands and then in having no sons to protect them and provide for them. As the famine continues, Naomi hears that there is food in Bethlehem. Naomi decides to return to her homeland and her husband's family. Elimelech owned land there, and perhaps she plans to sell it in order to provide for herself. She urges her daughters-in-law to return to their families so they will have people to support them; she will journey back to Bethlehem by herself. Maybe she feels the odds of making the journey safely are poor, and so she wants the younger women to stay in Moab. Both the younger women protest, but Naomi repeats her advice that they return to their families.

Orpah listens to Naomi and does as she asks, but Ruth refuses. This is the point when Ruth makes a declaration that is often quoted (out of context) in marriage ceremonies: "Entreat me not to leave thee, or to return from following after thee: for whither thou goest, I will go; and where thou lodgest, I will lodge: thy people shall be my people, and thy God my God: Where thou diest, will I die, and there will I be buried: the LORD do so to me, and more also, if aught but death part thee and me" (Ruth 1:16-17, KJV). For some reason, Ruth is willing to cast her lot with Naomi. She is willing to leave her relatives, her country, her culture, and her religion to travel into an unknown future with this woman to whom she has no blood ties. And she vows to stay with her for the rest of her life.

Ruth's remarkable declaration is even more striking because a single woman is casting her lot with another single woman whose lot is as uncertain as her own. Ruth commits herself to a lifelong tie to Naomi and claims Naomi's God and faith as her own. Then she says, "If I leave you, may the LORD do to me as to you, and even more" (Ruth 1:17, AP). In other words, "May God take my husband and sons as well, and even more, from me." Independence and courage of this sort show Ruth to be no ordinary woman. She exhibits great strength of character. But she is still an outsider, not even a Hebrew, not one of God's chosen people. Because Ruth is an outsider, her experience can be a window for each of us who also wonder how God can take notice of us and accept us.

The traditional theme of this second week of Advent is preparation, and usually we hear about John the Baptist, who quotes Isaiah, "Prepare ye the way of the LORD, make straight in the desert a highway for our God" (Isa. 40:3, KJV). We'll consider John's words later, but first let's examine the story of Ruth and Naomi in relation to that theme.

When Ruth and Naomi arrive in Bethlehem, the town buzzes with the news. Naomi has come back! When someone asks if she really is Naomi, returning after all these years, she responds, "Call me no longer Naomi, call me Mara" (which means "bitter") "for the Almighty has dealt bitterly with me. I went away full, but the LORD has brought me back empty." Naomi blames God, saying God has afflicted her in the deaths of her husband and sons. Soon everyone knows that Naomi has returned, bringing with her a young Moabite woman who has claimed the faith of Israel.

The two women have no money and no way to support themselves, but in Israel, landowners followed the custom of allowing the poor to glean in their fields. The needy could come through the fields behind the owner's harvesters, gathering the leftovers of the crop. Ruth goes into the barley fields outside Bethlehem to glean, in order to provide food for herself and Naomi. It happens that Ruth chooses a field belonging to Boaz, a wealthy kinsman of Elimelech's, Naomi's dead husband. It also happens that when Boaz comes out to the fields to check on the workers, he sees Ruth and asks who she is.

The servant in charge of the reapers tells him about Ruth's commitment to Naomi and about how hard Ruth has worked "from early this morning until now" (2:7) with little rest. Impressed, Boaz invites Ruth to eat with the reapers. Then Boaz instructs the servant to allow Ruth to glean as much as she likes and to deliberately drop some handfuls of grain for her to find. He also warns the young men working in the fields not to touch Ruth, indicating that he recognizes her vulnerability. With no husband, brothers, or father to protect her, Ruth could be at the mercy of these men. But Boaz assures Ruth that she will be safe and commends her for honoring Naomi and for acknowledging "the LORD, the God of Israel, under whose wings you have come for refuge" (Ruth 2:12). Boaz acts honorably, protecting and providing for this young woman who was married to his kinsman.

At the end of the day, Ruth has gathered a good deal of barley. When she goes home, Naomi asks where she has gleaned, in whose field. When Ruth tells Naomi that she has gleaned in the field belonging to Boaz and recounts how Boaz protected her and invited her back to glean with his workers, Naomi exclaims, "Blessed be he by the LORD, whose kindness has not forsaken the living or the dead!" In other words (translated into Southern), Naomi says, "The Lord bless his heart! He's done right by his kin!" And he had. Naomi explains to Ruth that Boaz is one of their "nearest kin." She instructs the young woman to follow Boaz's crew until the end of the harvest so that Boaz's workers never meet her in anyone else's field. Ruth does as she is told, working hard to gather enough barley to grind and sell, in order to support herself and her mother-in-law. And everyone notices. After all, the woman is young and a foreigner (and we can assume, apparently attractive, since Boaz takes care to warn his young men to leave her alone). But Naomi wants more than this for the younger woman. She says to Ruth, "My daughter, I need to seek some security for you, so that it may be well with you." And so Naomi comes up with a plan.

At the end of the barley harvest comes a celebration. When the time arrives, Naomi tells Ruth to bathe and perfume herself, then go to the threshing floor, where she will find Boaz. But Ruth is not to make her presence known. She is to hide herself until Boaz "shall have done eating and drinking" and to note the place where he chooses to sleep. Then she is to "uncover his feet" and to lie down beside him and wait to see what happens. So when Boaz "had eaten and drunk, and his heart was merry"—in other words, when he was drunk—Ruth "came softly, and uncovered his feet, and laid her down" (3:7, KJV). During the night, Boaz wakes with a start and finds a young woman lying beside him. He asks who she is, and Ruth tells him, saying, "Spread therefore thy skirt over thine handmaid, for thou art a near kinsman" (3:9, KJV). Asking Boaz to "spread his skirt over" her was probably an idiom for asking him to take her in, to take her under his protection. It is clear that Boaz takes Ruth's words to mean this. He praises her for not running after the young men but instead coming to him, and he promises to do right by her as Elimelech's kinsman, calling her "a virtuous woman." But he also tells her there is another kinsman, nearer than he and therefore with a stronger claim, who must first be given the opportunity to fulfill the role of kinsman redeemer.

Judging from the events that follow, Naomi and Boaz apparently understand each other. Both are clever and know how to use circumstances to their advantage. Boaz gives Ruth a present to take to Naomi, which suggests that he sees Naomi's hand in what has happened or at least that he desires her good will. When Naomi accepts the gift, she tells Ruth to sit tight, that before the day is over Boaz will act. Then Boaz goes to the city gate, where business is conducted, to wait for the nearer relative with the stronger claim on the land.

Selling the land owned by Naomi's husband, Elimelech, would be a last resort. A family held on to its land at all costs. If land had to be sold, it was offered first to family members. At the city gate, Boaz hails his relative when the man appears and gathers ten other men as his official witnesses. He says to the relative, "There's a parcel of land that belonged to our relative Elimelech. It is being offered for sale. If you want it, you have first claim. But if you don't want it, I'm next in line and I'm interested" (AP).

"I'll redeem it," the relative says.

Then Boaz adds, as if it were an afterthought (but of course we know it was not), "Oh, I forgot to mention that there's also the matter of the widow, Ruth the Moabitess. Whoever buys the land must marry her so she can have a son to carry on the name of our relative. That son will inherit the land later, of course." As you might imagine, this consideration changes the picture for the prospective kinsman redeemer. Apparently he is concerned about how a levirate marriage (remember this tradition from the story of Onan in chapter 1?) and children from it might complicate his life. Realizing that the property would not go to his existing heirs, the relative publicly relinquishes his claim on the land and on Ruth, stepping aside in favor of Boaz.

Here's where the story becomes like a fairy tale: Boaz marries Ruth, and soon they have a son, Obed. Naomi now has a grandson, heir to her sons' property, and she becomes Obed's nurse. The women of Bethlehem say to Naomi, who had called herself

"Mara"—the bitter one—that this child shall be "a restorer of life and a nourisher of your old age; for thy daughter-in-law who loves you, who is more to you than seven sons, has borne him" (Ruth 4:16). These two women, who have no home and no status, who have barely scraped by on the leavings of kind people, become a cherished wife and a cherished grandmother in a happy and honorable household. Can you see the difference in the two pictures of their circumstances? Naomi, the woman who declared that God had afflicted her, becomes a beloved grandmother with a daughter-in-law so loving that she is called better "than seven sons." Ruth, the stranger and outsider, the childless widow, becomes a chosen wife and mother.

Boaz finds love in his old age and becomes a father. Ruth and Boaz's son, Obed, becomes the father of Jesse, who becomes the father of David, and Jesus was "of the house and lineage of David." In fact, generations later Joseph will bring Mary to this same little town of Bethlehem to be counted in the census. But that's a story for another chapter.

PREPARING THE WAY

Returning to the theme of preparation, the machinations in the story of Ruth always make me think of Lucy Ricardo and Ethel Mertz trying to trick Ricky and Fred—and being found out and loved anyway in the end. Naomi is the scheming Lucy, and Ruth is the less astute but compliant and pure-hearted Ethel. Of course the story of Ruth is much more serious than an episode of *I Love Lucy*, but when I think of this week's Advent theme of preparation, I see these events in new ways.

Some interpreters of Ruth's story sanitize it, making all that goes on seem a part of a holy plan above mere human motives and needs. I don't see it quite that way. Naomi doesn't tell Ruth to hide herself on that threshing floor and wait for Boaz to pass out because Naomi believes God is up to something miraculous and is about to change their lives. Naomi thinks God has turned against her. The two women have been left on their own, and Naomi intends to do something about it by sending her daughter-in-law into the night. Ruth doesn't slip into bed alongside Boaz because she has heard heavenly voices telling her to do so. She does it because she knows Naomi well enough to know that this woman is a survivor, and she has cast her lot with Naomi. Boaz doesn't forget about Ruth in broaching the matter of the land sale to his relative; he has been flattered by the attentions of the young woman and wants her at least as much as he wants the land (which has never been offered for sale before that morning).

Then there's the matter of the euphemisms in Naomi's directions to Ruth. She tells Ruth to uncover Boaz's "feet." Hebrew writings often employ "feet" as a euphemism for genitals. Saying that Ruth slips under the covers alongside Boaz and uncovers his "feet" had a double meaning that would not have been lost on hearers of this story. When Boaz wakes and, startled, wonders aloud who the woman beside him is, the scene resembles a scene from a romantic comedy more than a biblical epic. These people do not seem to be aware of playing a role in a divine plan. They are simply being themselves. And there is nothing wrong with being completely human. So far in my life, I've yet to be anything more than human, and I don't know anyone else who has been so, either.

If we put ourselves into this story, we may see our lives and "preparing the way" this Advent in new ways. If we think of all that Naomi and Ruth experience and do as preparation for what God is going to do in the world, perhaps we can begin to see the events of our own lives as part of God's work too. We do not have to be conscious of a high and holy plan in order to be part of what God is doing. We may make poor and unwise choices and still be used by God.

Consider that Elimelech and Naomi leave Israel, the "Promised Land," and move to Moab. The land of Canaan was God's special gift to the people Israel, a land "flowing with milk and honey." Having milk meant raising dairy herds, and having honey meant keeping beehives, neither of which are highly portable. In other words, a land flowing with milk and honey was a settled land, a land where people stayed put. For the nomadic Hebrews who had wandered for forty years, such an image represented a great change. The name *Hebrew* (*ēevri* or *ivri* or *heevri*) comes from the Hebrew root word *avar* (*havar*), which means "to wander." So God's people are identified as wanderers by their very name. To be given a land, therefore, meant a change in their identity. In Canaan they had been given a place. They had permanent homes; they belonged. They would become a nation and be a light to other nations as those who worshiped the one true God. Going into the Promised Land meant receiving the good that God had promised and offered, and staying there meant experiencing fullness of life and God's blessings.

Moab, on the other hand, definitely is not the Promised Land. It is a place just outside the Promised Land. Moses stood and looked into the Promised Land from Moab. Although Moses had led the Hebrews out of Egypt, because of his disobedience he never entered Canaan. He was allowed only to see it from a distance. When we think of Moab in contrast to the Promised Land, Moab can represent all the times and ways we stop short of what God wants for us. It can represent all the times we leave what God wants or asks and settle for something less. In leaving Bethlehem and going to Moab, Naomi and Elimelech may have been attempting to satisfy their needs by their own efforts rather than trusting God. Moab could symbolize our chasing after what we think will satisfy us and leaving behind God's best for us in the process. Like Naomi and Elimelech, some people become Moabites by choice. That is, they consciously leave God behind and choose another way for themselves, ending up far from where God wants them. Other people, like Ruth, are Moabites by birth. They are born into settings where God is not worshiped or honored, and fullness of life is tough to find. I take great comfort in the fact that both Naomi and Ruth are welcomed to Bethlehem. Ruth the eager convert willingly leaves Moab and embraces God. Naomi the embittered widow returns reluctantly, having few options. Yet both find new life and hope. God embraces them both and transforms their lives.

All of Naomi and Ruth's experiences and all their actions become part of preparing a way for God to break into their lives and into the lives of others. I want to be clear: God does not send the loss, heartache, and shattered dreams that make their lives difficult. God does not operate in that way. God wills only good for us, and God wants fullness of life for each of us. But in this fallen and imperfect world, God acts as both an opportunist and an efficiency expert. God the opportunist uses our smallest desire for more, the tiniest chink in our armor of self-sufficiency to reach into our lives in love. God the efficiency expert lets nothing go to waste. Nothing that happens to us is ever lost. In God's ecosystem, everything in our lives, even the worst experiences, can teach us about eternal love and draw us toward God's purposes. Those episodes can prepare us to be where we need to be and mold us into people whom God can use.

Circumstances and relationships prepare these two women, and generations later, others who have roles in the Christmas story. Someone and some set of experiences mold Joseph into a man of kindness and compassion who resolves to put Mary away quietly rather than to disgrace her by a public divorce. Someone teaches him to listen to God so that when the dreams come, he changes his mind about divorcing Mary. In a similar way, someone helps Mary to grow into a young woman willing to say yes to God. Someone nurtures in her a faith strong enough that she can believe God will perform miracles. Years before Jesus is born, God is preparing people and circumstances. God is preparing Mary and Joseph to make the journey to Bethlehem.

In a similar way, all our experiences are part of preparing us for our journey toward God. The moment we turn toward our Bethlehem, toward what God is calling us to be and to do, God's power cooperates fully with our desire. Even before that moment, according to John Wesley's theology, God works in us to create the desire that launches us on the journey. Before we are even conscious of God's activity in the world and in us, God the opportunist uses our every impulse toward wholeness to inch into our thoughts and our lives. God is at work preparing us and "preparing the way" before we even realize there's a journey to be made.

Once we decide to begin the journey, once we realize that we want to clear the road between us and God—well, then, things really start to happen. The call to make that decision is the call to preparation we hear during Advent. On the second Sunday, we usually read in worship John the Baptist's words, "Make straight the way of the Lord" (John 1:23), and Isaiah's call to "make . . . a highway for our God" (Isa. 40:3). My pastor, Howard Olds, told a story about his father that helped me to think of this call in a new way. The elder Mr. Olds, a man of few words, could improve Howard and his brother's behavior by looking at them and saying quietly and directly one simple phrase: "Straighten up." That in essence is the message of John and of Isaiah: "Straighten up. Mend your ways. Clear away anything that stands between you and God." Clearing the path is sometimes clearly necessary.

Psalm 85:13 speaks of righteousness going before us to prepare the way. We receive and perceive God more easily—the way is smoother and more direct—when we are trying to live rightly. It's sort of like walking through a field of tall weeds (and life sometimes is a veritable thicket) and having someone go before us to mash down the grass. Progress is simply easier when someone has gone before and prepared the way. Similarly, God can get through to us more readily—to reach us and speak to us—when we position ourselves to listen and look for God's coming. We position ourselves to hear and see God when we read the Bible, worship, pray, and just pause in our busyness during this hectic time of year.

Even if there are no "big" sins standing in our way, we can still make the way smoother. Activities like reading this book and attending Advent study groups can help us to clear a path to God. Spending time with the reflection questions and journaling can help us to clear out a space in our minds and hearts by making time in our schedules for God. Sitting quietly in God's presence can help us to experience God's welcoming love in the midst of a world that sometimes is not so welcoming.

The prophets remind us of our part in preparing for God's coming this Advent. They ask us to look at our lives and clear away anything that stands in the way of our giving attention to God. This Advent, God calls us to come home for Christmas. God calls us to come back from all those places where we have settled for less than the fullness of life promised to us in Christ. God calls us back from all the ambitions and possessions we have pursued, thinking they would satisfy us. God calls us to let go of any bitterness and resistance to forgive that block the light of love from warming us. Preparing for Christmas means looking deep within ourselves and asking if our hearts are truly at home in the lives we are living. God calls us to come home and to rest, to be embraced by one who loves us as we are. God offers us a place where we are fully known and also fully accepted.

God has been placing this offer before us since before we were even interested. God has been at work not just in what we would call overtly religious ways but also through ordinary actions and embedded traditions in our lives. For instance, Israel's tradition of the kinsman redeemer was a vehicle of grace in place long before Ruth and Naomi made the journey to Bethlehem, and the tradition of gleaning laid the groundwork to keep them alive day by day. Ruth's willingness to work hard and take risks characterized her personality, but they also expressed God's intent to supply Naomi's needs. God had shaped Boaz's honorable character to make him a man of compassion who protected Ruth and who, by following tradition, allowed the childless widow to have a home. Ruth's relationship with Naomi brought Ruth from another country to warm Boaz's life. Their son became the means for God to melt the bitterness in Naomi's heart. God used all these circumstances. Even if the people involved thought they were acting completely on their own initiative, God was at work.

In a similar way, God is also at work to prepare us to open ourselves to love. God uses all that happens to us, all our less-than-what-God-wants choices. The One we seek is at work in ways we can't even recognize, guiding us toward the path by which to make our way home.

The answer to Ruth's question points to a deep truth of Advent. "Why have I found favor in your sight?" she asks. Why indeed? The amazing truth for all of us is that we have "found favor" with God not because of who we are but because of who God is. As Peter wrote, we who were "not a people" have become "God's people" (1 Pet. 2:10). We have been claimed by God, from whom, the Letter to the Ephesians tells us, "every family in heaven and on earth takes its [true] name" (Eph. 3:15). We who did not have a place, we who were the last ones chosen for the team, we who looked longingly at those in the "in" crowd, we who never quite measured up, we who were outsiders, have "found favor." God claims us, and we have a part in what God is doing. From the beginning of time, according to Romans 8, God has been preparing us and preparing to meet us in this relationship. God takes notice of us in whatever field where we are gleaning, calling us from whatever we are doing to "get by," and makes us a member of the family. And it is not just any family; it is the family through whom God comes into the world, again and again. As amazing as that seems, Ruth's story shows us that it is true.

REFLECTION PAGES

DAY 1 REFLECTION

Read Ruth 1:1-18.

Reflect.

Think of people you have known, who, like Naomi, felt that the "hand of the LORD" had gone against them. Why do you think some people feel that way while others with similar losses or difficulties do not?

_____
_____
_____
_____
_____
_____
_____
_____
_____

Something made Ruth willing to leave her home, her family, her culture, and her religion to go with Naomi. Yet Naomi described herself as a bitter person who felt that God had turned against her. How might you explain Ruth's love for this bitter woman?

_____
_____
_____
_____
_____
_____
_____
_____
_____

Imagine that you are Orpah, watching Naomi and Ruth depart. What do you want to say to them as they leave?

_____
_____
_____
_____

When have you made a decision that required turning your back on a place or experience in your past in order to move into the future you felt God wanted for you? Were you aware at the time that you were doing something important? Is there anything that you want or need to leave behind this Christmas season?

_____

_____

_____

_____

_____

_____

_____

_____

Rest.

Think of all the people around the world who are refugees, having left their homes because of hardship there. Hold these people before God and ask God to be with them.

Pray a breath prayer.

Until your next reflection time, pray a breath prayer on behalf of people who are traveling. You may mention particular people or pray a prayer such as this, "O God, be with those traveling today."

DAY 2 REFLECTION

Read Ruth 2:8-20.

Reflect.

Consider Boaz's actions. What do you think motivated him to be kind to Ruth?

_____

_____

_____

The tradition of allowing gleaners was a way of providing for the poor. In what traditions that provide for the poor have you participated?

Which Christmas traditions do you enjoy most? Why?

Which Christmas traditions do you participate in most regularly? Why? Do you participate in any Christmas traditions that you don't enjoy? Why or why not?

_____

_____

_____

_____

_____

_____

_____

_____

_____

_____

_____

_____

_____

_____

_____

_____

_____

Rest.
Think of those with whom you will be spending the holidays. Picture what the meetings will be like and envision God present with you in those encounters.

Pray a breath prayer.
Pray a breath prayer for those who are in need as Christmas approaches, such as, "O God, comfort those in need."

DAY 3 REFLECTION

Read Ruth 2:21-3:18.

Reflect.

Judging from the events described in these verses, Naomi is something of a schemer. What do you think of her? If you compared her to a fictional character, whom would you say she is like?

Imagine Ruth getting ready to go to the threshing floor. What do you think she is feeling and thinking about?

Boaz is an honorable man who is apparently concerned with guarding Ruth's reputation, but he doesn't ask her to leave when he wakes up and finds her beside him. How does this behavior fit with the rest of his actions?

Boaz takes notice of Ruth because of her kindness toward her mother-in-law and her hard work. What traits do you think people would mention in describing your close relationships?

_____
_____
_____
_____
_____
_____
_____
_____
_____
_____
_____
_____
_____
_____
_____
_____
_____
_____
_____
_____
_____
_____
_____
_____

Rest.

Sit in God's presence and give thanks for the life skills and good attitudes that you learned from the people who surrounded you in your early life.

Pray a breath prayer.

Compose a breath prayer about those who have led you or pray, "God of life, thank you for those who formed me."

DAY 4 REFLECTION

Read Ruth 4:1-18.

Reflect.

Do you know someone like Naomi, someone whose life seems to have turned around completely, from despair to joy? What happened? Do you and that person see God at work in the changes?

This passage links Ruth and Boaz and their son with Tamar and Judah's sons in Genesis. What connection do you see between the stories? What events are similar? How is God involved in and mentioned in each story?

Imagine that you are Naomi, explaining to the little boy Obed how his dad and mom came to be married. How would you weave God's working into the story?

Looking back at your own life, consider whether God brought you into important relationships that molded you and changed the direction of your life. How has God intervened in your life?

_____

_____

_____

_____

_____

_____

_____

_____

_____

_____

_____

_____

_____

Rest.

Sit quietly and imagine God looking at you as Naomi looked at her grandson, Obed. Feel God's delight in you. Think about how God welcomes you. Stay as long as you like.

Pray a breath prayer.

For a breath prayer until your next time of reflection, pray in gratitude, "Thank you, God, for accepting me."

DAY 5 REFLECTION

Read Matthew 1:18-25.

Reflect.
Think about Joseph's deciding to deal privately with Mary rather than to denounce her publicly and about his accepting responsibility for a child that was not his. What experiences and influences do you suppose formed him into such a compassionate person?

Who have you known like Joseph—kind, quietly faithful, reflective, good, compassionate? What experiences do you think shaped them to be so?

God spoke to Joseph in a dream. What dreams do you remember? Have you ever asked God whether your dreams had special meaning? Do you think dreams can bring guidance about life's problems? Why or why not?

What experiences in your life have prepared you to want to listen to God? What people are models for you of how to listen to God?

_____

_____

_____

_____

_____

_____

Rest.

Sit in God's presence and reflect on people who have taught you how to listen to God. Listen for anything God may want to say to you.

Pray a breath prayer.

Until your next time of reflection, pray a breath prayer of your own creation or this one: "God of many paths, draw me close to you."

CHAPTER 3

THE WONDER OF BEING SOUGHT: WHY HAS THIS HAPPENED TO ME?

O most merciful Redeemer,

. . . .

may we know thee more clearly,

love thee more dearly,

and follow thee more nearly,

day by day.

—Richard of Chichester

thirteenth century

A couple of holy people they are, Zechariah and Elizabeth. Luke's Gospel tells us, "Both of them were righteous before God, living blamelessly according to all the commandments and regulations of the Lord" (Luke 1:6). Since hundreds of regulations in addition to the Ten Commandments governed righteous living, that is a remarkable character reference. Zechariah and Elizabeth are "righteous" and live "blamelessly." Both are descended from priestly lines. Describing a woman's ancestry is unusual in the Bible. Even in the case of Jesus, we are told only Joseph's heritage—"of the house and lineage of David." We aren't told whether Mary descended from any noted line.

Priestly heritage and faithfulness have not protected Elizabeth and Zechariah from the sorrow of childlessness, however. When Elizabeth finally becomes pregnant, she states, "This is what the Lord has done for me when he looked favorably on me and took away the disgrace I have endured among my people" (Luke 1:25). She has "endured" disgrace because of her barrenness. When Elizabeth married Zechariah, she probably prepared a layette for their first child as any woman would. Can you picture her making tiny clothes and accumulating them?

But as years pass and no children are born, Elizabeth stops preparing for motherhood. She puts the clothes away or perhaps gives them to a younger relative. She resigns herself to the pity, scorn, and speculation of those who wonder what she and Zechariah have done to deserve this sad fate. She endures disgrace.

Then something wondrous happens: Late in life Elizabeth conceives. The one person who could have prepared her for the surprise is Zechariah, but as we know from the first chapter, he has been stricken speechless because he questioned an angel messenger. Since women were not educated at that time, even if he had written her a note, she could not have read it. The undoubtedly surprised Elizabeth secludes herself, probably waiting until she can be sure that she is indeed pregnant. After all, she might not be. She could be entering menopause or have some illness. At other times over the years she may have thought she was pregnant; she will not go public until she knows the pregnancy is certain. In those days no home pregnancy tests could confirm or dash her hopes. She will be sure only at quickening, when she feels the child move within her. Since this is Elizabeth's first pregnancy, she may not be sure that those first mild flutterings are indeed a baby's movement. Perhaps she has been mistaken about that before too. So she remains in seclusion, telling no one but probably hugging herself with joy as she becomes more certain that her disgrace is about to end.

Then the angel tells someone else about Elizabeth's child—Mary. Mary travels to the hill country of Judea to visit her aging cousin, who is in the sixth month of pregnancy. When Mary enters and speaks, Elizabeth's child does not merely move; the Bible says that the baby "leaps" in his mother's womb. There can be no mistaking the source of the sensation now, even for the uninitiated Elizabeth.

I have tried to imagine Elizabeth's joy. I remember my own excitement when I finally became pregnant after many months of tests and procedures. For us it took a few years; for Elizabeth and Zechariah it has been many years. They had given up on their dream. Elizabeth's joy is the joy of a life changed by God's unexpected touch. From my own experience and those of others in my family, I know that news of a long-awaited baby brings rejoicing. Years ago I heard a television report about a survey of women that asked them to name the happiest day of their life. Before the announcer could continue, I (a relatively new mother myself) guessed out loud, "The day their first child was born." And that was the most common answer. For a woman who wants a child, there is no greater joy than giving birth to that baby. So Elizabeth has reason for joy. But her joy is not only because of her own pregnancy. Suddenly, when Mary enters her home, Elizabeth knows that Mary is also pregnant and that she will one day call Mary's child "my Lord."

Though the fact is seldom noted, it seems Elizabeth is the first person to realize on her own that Mary is pregnant and the first to proclaim from her own insight that Christ is about to enter the world. The others learn the news by way of an angel's visit or a dream. But Elizabeth knows from an inward witness, and she boldly announces that Mary's child will be the Messiah. As far as I can tell from the stories in the Gospels, she is also the first person to confirm publicly what the angel told Mary. Imagine what a relief it must have been to Mary to have Elizabeth as an encourager. Scripture also singles out Elizabeth in describing her as "filled with the Holy Spirit," the only woman so characterized. The angel Gabriel tells Mary that the Holy Spirit will "come upon her," but even Mary is not described as "filled with" the Holy Spirit. That description is reserved for Elizabeth. All of us who have "finally" received a great blessing or gift can celebrate Elizabeth and celebrate with her.

CHOSEN FOR RELATIONSHIP

On the third Sunday of Advent, the Sunday of joy, we acknowledge the excitement of the promise fulfilled. Elizabeth's story illustrates this theme beautifully. God tells Zechariah through an angel's visit that he and his wife will know the joy of having a child, but Elizabeth comes to that knowledge without an angel or a dream or any special sign to help her believe. She knows the incredible joy of having her disgrace wiped away, but she also experiences the added joy of recognizing that God is about to do something even more wonderful, and not just for her and Zechariah personally but for the whole world. She realizes that the Messiah is about to be born.

Elizabeth asks Mary, "Why has this happened to me, that the mother of my Lord comes to me?" Her question reflects the wonder of realizing that God comes to us individually. And that reality is remarkable. God could herd us all together like flocks of sheep and redeem us in groups. God could zap whole congregations and speed up the process of saving the world. But God wants relationship with each of us and so chooses to come to us one by one. The relationships described in the stories about Tamar and Rahab are business arrangements in which people strike a deal and trust one another only minimally. In Ruth's story, we witness relationship in the course of ordinary human interactions when a benevolent relative, Boaz, notices Ruth. But in Elizabeth's story we see relationship of a different order.

Elizabeth is overwhelmed when she realizes that the mother of the Messiah has come to her personally. A righteous and blameless person, she finds that fact of being sought by God difficult to grasp and impossible to explain. We ordinary folks who intimately know ourselves to be less than righteous and less than blameless find it even more difficult to understand that God seeks us out and wants relationship with us! Because relationships are built one person at a time, God invests time and energy in each one of us, knowing each one of us is unique and infinitely valuable.

In Elizabeth we can observe a truth about God's ways with us. Elizabeth and Zechariah are living their accustomed lives in a little hill town, being quietly faithful to God. She is being a wife, and he is serving in the temple as priestly families did in those times—when it comes his turn, in the usual course of events. On that day when the angel comes to him in the temple, Zechariah has been selected by lot to enter the sanctuary and light the incense. He has not been selected because of any personal achievement; it is simply his turn. Elizabeth is not in the public eye; she is not a prominent person. Yet even though she does not leave her home, God comes to her. "Why has this happened to me?" she asks Mary. Why, indeed? Why would God choose an obscure woman like Elizabeth to first publicly proclaim the truth about Jesus' nature? Elizabeth's relationship with Mary offers a clue.

We are not told what Mary is thinking or why she comes to visit Elizabeth. Perhaps Mary comes simply to help her cousin. Once Mary knows that Elizabeth is pregnant, she probably realizes that she would appreciate company. I like to think a special relationship between the two women makes Mary feel she could and should go to Elizabeth. Perhaps Elizabeth, the childless one, has been like a special aunt to Mary all her life. Perhaps Mary has made this trip to the hill country of Judea many times. Perhaps she has gone there as eagerly and as often as I went to my grandma and grandpa's on weekends when I was a child. Maybe it was the priest Zechariah and his godly wife, Elizabeth, who taught Mary about the promised Messiah. Maybe she holds cherished memories of being in their home. For whatever reason, when Mary finds herself pregnant, she goes to Elizabeth. And she stays with her for three months. Mary's parents are never mentioned, and her long visit with Elizabeth makes me believe there was a special closeness between these two. Mary's mother may not have been living. Though the Bible does not explicitly say so, I like to think that Mary is with Elizabeth until John was born. Elizabeth is in her sixth month of pregnancy when Mary comes, and Mary stays three months. I can't imagine that she'd leave when Elizabeth is nine months pregnant, without waiting to see that Elizabeth and the baby are well. No, I think Mary is there when John the Baptist is born. And she stays for good reason.

We hear a clue to the reason in Elizabeth's greeting to Mary. Elizabeth says, "Blessed are you among women, and blessed is the fruit of your womb. . . . And blessed is she who believed that there would be a fulfillment of what was spoken to her by the Lord" (Luke 1:42, 45). Mary is young, unmarried, and pregnant, and her cousin calls her "blessed." Three times, in fact, Elizabeth uses that word. Not only that, Elizabeth knows and acknowledges that something rare and incredible is going on through this young woman. We know that Mary was frightened by her encounter with the angel; perhaps the content of the angel's message has become even more frightening to Mary in her solitude once the angel left. Perhaps she needs reassurance and someone to talk to. In any case, she comes to Elizabeth, and Elizabeth receives her, not with suspicions and censure but with affirmation. I imagine them having long talks about how amazing God is. Elizabeth is great with child and getting on in years, so she probably is not physically active. I'm sure the two have lots of time to talk.

I can almost hear Elizabeth reassuring the younger woman, helping her to accept the miracle that is happening. After all, Elizabeth is experiencing something almost like a miracle herself, after her years of childlessness. I believe Mary stays because she needs Elizabeth; she needs to hear Elizabeth's blessing and feel Elizabeth's affirmation of her. That blessing and affirmation strengthen Mary to face what lies ahead. Just as we all need someone in difficult times, Mary needs someone to help her hang on to what God has promised. She is going into uncharted territory, and her only reassurance is the memory of an angel's visit months earlier. But Elizabeth affirms that Mary is "blessed."

It is difficult to overstate the power of blessing one another and naming one another as blessed by God. The Bible offers us multiple stories of sons who seek their fathers' blessings. The well-known story of Jacob and Esau implies this blessing is worth lying and scheming for; the loss of it is enough to make Esau want to kill his brother. A father's blessing of the eldest son was a powerful act. In our less structured, modern interactions, parents' words have great power in the lives of their children, even though parents may not impart a formal blessing. Often parents do not realize the influence they have. When parents say, "Johnny is our creative one" or, "Susie is a natural athlete," they may not realize that they are forming Johnny for a career in art or that Susie will expend great energy in developing her tennis stroke, all because they overhear their parents. The words we speak have power, and when we speak a blessing, we act powerfully.

My favorite benediction from Hebrew scripture evokes a beautiful image of the power in a blessing. The blessing comes from the Book of Numbers (6:24-26):

> The LORD bless you and keep you;
> the LORD make his face to shine upon you, and be gracious unto you;
> the LORD lift up his countenance upon you, and give you peace.

God says further to Moses, "So they shall put my name on the Israelites, and I will bless them" (Num. 6:27). When we bless another in the name of God, when we "put [God's] name on" someone, we ask God to turn toward them. We bid the light that emanates from God's face to shine upon them. We bring the power of God's light into their circumstances. This benediction is echoed in the prayer of Psalm 4:6: "Let the light of your face shine on us, O LORD!"

In the South, we have informally incorporated the act of blessing one another into our daily lives. It shows up often in our speech. A friend of mine told me what his grandmother used to say when she held any of her grandchildren on her knee: "Bless your heart, my darling. Bless your heart. I'm just so proud [glad] to see you." He went on to say, "It was a blessing that has followed me all the days and years since then."

My grandma was such a person for me, too, during those weekends I spent with her and my grandpa. To this day I remember the love and delight in her face and in her voice as she greeted me. After I became an adult, she said to me during one of our visits, "I know I'm not supposed to have favorites, but you were always my favorite. You know that, don't you?" And I believed her. Now I also concede that she, like the mother in *Prince of Tides*, may have told all my siblings and cousins that each was her favorite, but that doesn't matter to me. What matters is that when she put her arms around me and hugged me to her, I felt loved and safe and special. I felt *blessed*, even though I didn't know to use that word for the feeling. I credit the love and affirmation I received from my grandma with nurturing in me what I call my "center of wellness"—that part of me that pulls me toward health and wholeness and enables me to care for myself. She loved me and blessed me with her affirming words, and that love still follows me and draws me toward the fullness of life that God offers. Even before I had a conscious desire to know God, the love my grandma poured into my life prepared me to understand and respond to God's love when it was identified for me. Returning to the image from the last chapter, she "prepared the way" for me to respond to God's love.

I hope someone in your life has conferred similar blessing upon you, because those positive words do follow us. Our words have the power to shape others' perceptions of themselves in life-changing ways. We can strengthen them to follow God, and in the process, experience God's presence ourselves. To bless one another is to affirm each individual's loveliness to God. But words also have power for the opposite effect. They can limit and control. Consider the power of negative words.

Years ago a friend told me his family members repeatedly said to him, "You'll never amount to anything." I cannot understand why any family would continually say such a thing, but the people in his family did. Haunted by those negative words, he became determined to prove them wrong. "I'll show them" became the watchword of his life. In spite of great odds, he found a way to go to college. Then he got a good job. He put his energy into achieving and earning, determined to "show them." In middle age, he found himself captive by work and the desire to win others' praise. He was successful, but then the unthinkable happened: He lost his job. Overnight, the life he had worked so hard to build, crumbled; he was in crisis. Only his success had made him someone. Without the job that had become his outward proof of worth, he was adrift. As months passed without his finding another job, he plunged into despair. His family's words had the power of a curse, and he felt himself to be nothing. At this critical time, someone in his church invited him to join a group of men who met weekly to support one another in their Christian journey. Slowly, through the power of their friendship and their prayers, he realized that he had been controlled by a lie. His friends helped him to see that he was much more than what he earned, much more than his job. But he could not free himself of the lie about success until he traced his obsession back to its origins and understood what had been driving him. With the help of the men who supported him, my friend realized that God did not name him a failure but with a new name: "Beloved and blessed—just as you are." To bless someone by naming that person in relation to God and what God is doing in the world can make a tremendous difference!

Most of us do not take time to uncover negative messages from the past that limit us. Most of us do not have dramatic insights such as my friend had. But we all remember both positive and negative words. Maybe you had a label in your family—"the studious one," "the athletic one," "the funny one," "the chubby one," "the clumsy one"—that still shapes or limits how you think about yourself or that causes you pain or self-doubt. Labels can haunt us. Mary surely had moments when she wondered if the townspeople would say terrible things about her and Joseph and even the child, once he was born. After all, by law Joseph should put her away for adultery since she was pregnant, unless the baby was his, which would make both of them subject to censure. How was she going to make it through the months of her pregnancy, with no one knowing or understanding what was happening? I can imagine her repeating to herself many times Elizabeth's words, "Blessed are you among women." Words, just words. But I think Mary needed those "just words."

I have experienced the sustaining power of supportive words myself; I know how important they can be. Years ago when I was going through my divorce, I was in graduate school. A kind and observant professor lingered after class one day to ask if I was okay. Somehow he had sensed my distress. I explained that my husband and I had separated and were divorcing. He told me he was sorry that I was going through this pain, and then he added, "But I know God has a rich and full future ahead for you." Those words came back to me time and time again through the months that followed. When depression seemed about to overwhelm me, his compassionate, hope-filled words would echo in my spirit as a life-giving blessing. I wasn't able to believe them for myself, but knowing that he believed them for me was a great gift. He blessed me with those few words spoken in compassion. That I still remember them after so many years is proof of their power. We all have the power to bless others with our words, to speak truth that can sustain them through many dark days and nights. You probably can recall such words from your own life. They both carry and shape us. Knowing that helps me to appreciate Elizabeth's role in Mary's life.

Elizabeth, staying in her quiet town, waiting for her baby to be born, realizes that the great God of the universe has touched her life and is coming to all the world. It seems too incredible to be true. But she proclaims to Mary and to us that it is true. "Oh well," we say, "maybe God caused Elizabeth to say what she did as a special gift for Mary. She was Jesus' mother, after all." But one lesson I draw from Elizabeth's wondering question is that God does indeed come to ordinary people. God is active on both sides of the equation: God comes to us in those who bless us, and God comes to others through us when we bless them.

While messages from God came through and to particular women and men, the Bible tells us that no prophecy is "of any private interpretation" (2 Pet. 1:20, KJV). That is, the truths of the Bible's words go beyond these few people in specific places. The truths throughout the Bible belong to each of us. Its truths about God's nature and God's ways of dealing with people in these stories speak to and can guide all of us. That is the special sense in which every verse in the Bible is true for each of us. Even though Mary and Elizabeth had specific roles to play in a particular place and time, they are a part of the promise made centuries earlier to Abraham: "By your offspring shall all the nations of the earth gain blessing" (Gen. 22:18). Similarly, even though Jesus was born in a specific time and place, his coming is also personal and timeless, for each of us.

Elizabeth's experience reminds us that God does come to humans like us. Through prophets and priests and friends and relatives, God claims us and tells us that we are loved and worth loving. But we have short memories. We all forget those truths, and so we are given the privilege of reminding one another over and over. The grieving person needs someone to say, "You are not alone. I care, and God cries with you and is holding you close." The child struggling in school needs someone to say, "You are a wonderful person. You are a gift from God, and I am so glad you're here." The teenager wracked with self-doubt needs someone to say, "You have wonderful gifts to share with the world, and I am proud of you." The tired worker needs someone to say, "You do a good job, and I appreciate your effort." In as many ways as there are people, we need to say to one another from the heart, "Blessed are you. God comes into the world through you." Such words can be God's healing touch for whatever disgrace someone may have endured, for whatever censure someone may have received for not living up to others' expectations.

We find words of blessing throughout the Bible. When Jesus is baptized, God speaks from heaven, saying, "You are my Son, the Beloved; with you I am well pleased" (Mark 1:11). That statement echoes words recorded in Isaiah: "'Here is my servant, whom I have chosen, my beloved, / with whom my soul is well pleased'" (Isa. 42:1). In the words *chosen, beloved, well pleased* we witness God blessing Jesus as Elizabeth did Mary. We are made in God's image, and so there is power in our words as well, power to bless one another and even to bless God. Many of the psalms offer us patterns for blessing. Psalm 103 makes it a refrain:

> Bless the LORD, O my soul,
>   and all that is within me,
>   bless his holy name.

Bless the LORD, O my soul,
>> and do not forget all his benefits—
who forgives . . . ,
>> who heals . . . ,
who redeems. . . .

—Psalm 103:1-4

In many prayers, we say, "We bless your holy name, O God," without considering why we do it. I believe we can learn a deep truth here about why blessing one another through our words is so important. We think of God as complete, needing nothing from us. But what if God needs our "blessing"? What if God needs our acknowledgment of the holiness and worth of our Creator, just as we hunger to be completely known and completely loved? What if, at the center of the universe, the fount of all creation, all life, is the yearning to be known, loved, affirmed, embraced—the yearning to be chosen and claimed in loving relationship? What if that desire for affirmation and acceptance lies at the center of all that is? Does God need to be blessed by us? Certainly God does not need us in the same sense that humans need food, shelter, breath. But maybe somehow, at the deepest level of reality, God needs us. Why did God create humanity? In order to be in relationship with us. Considering the need to be known and blessed in relationship may bring us closer to the heart of the Advent message. In Christ God comes to each of us, to offer each of us the only relationship that can truly satisfy, and through Christ we find relationship with God, who yearns from the beginning of time to be loved by us, to be close to us.

Why should God come to us, ordinary as we are, and claim us as chosen? Scripture gives us the answer repeatedly: because God who created us also steadily loves us and delights in us (see Gen. 1:31; Ps. 18:19; Isa. 42:1; 62:4; John 3:16; Rom. 5:8; 1 John 4:9). Tamar and Rahab show us partnership, a relationship built on what people can do for one another. Ruth shows us the relationship of a benevolent relative who recognizes our need when we show up. God uses such relationships, but God wants more than those alliances. But Elizabeth's words remind us that God's love is not a benign, detached love waiting for us to take the first step. God *is* love, and God is active love that seeks us out. "Why has this happened to me?" Elizabeth wonders. God's active love is the answer, and it is the reason for our joy during Advent.

Reflection Pages

Day 1 Reflection

Read Luke 1:5-7.

Reflect.

Think about one or two people whom you would describe as "righteous before God." What traits and attitudes describe them? How are they different from one another?

_____

_____

_____

_____

_____

_____

_____

Which of the traits and behaviors that you listed above most challenge you to greater faithfulness? Which ones are you growing in?

_____

_____

_____

_____

_____

_____

Elizabeth and Zechariah were "getting on in years." It was almost too late for them to become parents. Do you feel it is too late in your life to do or accomplish some things? What dreams that you once held on to do you now think may not come to reality?

_____

_____

_____

_____

_____

_____

_____

_____

What dreams from earlier years have come true for you? Having a home and family? Getting a particular job? Learning a skill?

_____

_____

Rest.

Think of some older saints, people you know who are "getting on in years." Hold them before God in prayer, in gratitude for their faithfulness and their example. Consider how you can let them know the importance of their role in your community of faith.

Pray a breath prayer.

For a breath prayer until your next time of reflection, consider praying, "God of dreams, fill me with excitement."

DAY 2 REFLECTION

Read Luke 1:8-20.

Reflect.

Zechariah was chosen by lot to offer incense in the temple. What tasks seem to have fallen to you within your community of faith? How do you feel about those tasks? Are they joys or merely responsibilities?

Imagine what it would be like to be surprised by an angel as the people of God were praying just outside your door. About what dream or situation would you ask the angel for guidance?

_____

_____

_____

_____

_____

_____

_____

_____

_____

The angel told Zechariah that the child John would be born in spite of Zechariah's unbelief. Have you ever doubted that a promise of God's would be kept and then been surprised by God's faithfulness? When has God been more faithful to you than you were able to be in return?

What messages or promises from God are you treasuring and seeing come true in your life?

_____

_____

_____

_____

_____

_____

_____

_____

_____

_____

_____

_____

_____

Rest.

Sit in God's presence and consider your role in your community of faith. Feel God's gratitude for the ways you are faithful. Be open to what God may show you about future roles as well as current ones.

Pray a breath prayer.

For a breath prayer until your next time of reflection, consider praying, "Faithful God, make me faithful."

DAY 3 REFLECTION

Read Luke 1:24-25, 39-45.

Reflect.

Elizabeth said, "This is what the Lord has done for me." Think back on some times of joy in your life. What has God done for you that you celebrate?

_____

_____

_____

_____

_____

_____

What has God done for you recently? Where do you see reason for joy in the world? in your life?

_____

_____

_____

_____

_____

_____

What people have been Elizabeths for you, people you could go to in times of crisis? What did they do that helped you and allowed you to go to them?

_____

_____

_____

_____

_____

_____

For whom have you been privileged to be an Elizabeth, a reliable friend who shared faith and encouragement?

_____

_____

_____

_____

_____

_____

Who has helped you to identify or pay attention to God's work in your life?

_____

_____

_____

Rest.

Look back on your friendships with awareness of God's work. How has God used your friendships to shape you in faithfulness? How have you been a friend in faith for others?

Pray a breath prayer.

For a breath prayer until your next time of reflection, consider praying, "Friend and Brother Christ, thank you for being with me."

DAY 4 REFLECTION

Read Luke 1:45, 50.

Reflect.

Think of someone whose support has helped to strengthen your faith. Draft here a note of thanks to that person, even if she or he is no longer living or you have lost touch. If it is possible, mail or deliver the note as a gift before Christmas.

_____

_____

_____

_____

_____

_____

_____

Whose love and acceptance have helped you to know what it feels like to be called "blessed"? What words and actions of those individuals do you remember?

With what child or young person can you establish an ongoing relationship of blessing? Who needs a loving friend that you can be?

Think of two or three people with whom you spend time regularly. In what way does each one need reassurance and "blessing"? How can you convey God's love to each one in your interactions?

_____

_____

_____

_____

_____

_____

_____

_____

_____

_____

_____

_____

_____

_____

_____

_____

_____

_____

_____

_____

Rest.

Listen as God says to you, "You are blessed and precious to me. I am with you." What does this message mean to you today?

Pray a breath prayer.

For a breath prayer until your next time of reflection, consider praying, "O God, I bless your name."

DAY 5 REFLECTION

Read Mark 1:9-11.

Reflect.

Sit quietly and picture John and Jesus standing in the Jordan River. What feelings does the scene suggest to you?

_____

_____

_____

_____

_____

Imagine what it looked and sounded like when the heavens opened and God spoke. Describe what you imagine.

_____

_____

_____

_____

Imagine yourself standing alongside Jesus in the water as God says, including you, "You are my beloved." Let God's words flow over you. What do you feel?

_____

_____

_____

_____

_____

What individuals do you know who need to realize that they are precious to God and beloved? How can you help them to experience this truth?

_____

_____

_____

_____

_____

_____

Rest.

With your finger, trace the sign of the cross on your forehead or in your palm. Sit quietly and allow God to say to you, "You are my beloved. I delight in you."

Pray a breath prayer.

For a breath prayer until your next time of reflection, consider praying, "Holy God, thank you for loving me."

CHAPTER 4

WRESTLING WITH MYSTERY: HOW CAN THIS BE?

. . . have patience with everything unresolved in your heart and . . . try to love the questions themselves. . . . the point is, to live everything. Live the questions now. Perhaps then, someday far in the future, you will gradually, without even noticing it, live your way into the answer.

—Rainer Maria Rilke

Letters to a Young Poet

The angel Gabriel doesn't get to sit on a cloud and play the harp much during the events we celebrate at Christmas. He stays busy, appearing to various people in different places with messages about the incredible things God is about to do. Many times when angels appear in the Bible, the first words they speak are, "Fear not." The angels say this to Zechariah and to the shepherds. This standard conversation opener tells us there must be something overwhelming about angels. People become terrified when these beings appear. In fact, the word *terrified* is used to describe both Zechariah and the shepherds. The appearance of angels means that God is on the move, that big things are happening, that change is afoot. Even without an angelic messenger, that news would cause fear in many of us.

But Gabriel opens the conversation with Mary by saying, "Greetings, favored one," which perplexes the young girl. In the ensuing conversation, the angel tells Mary she will soon bear a child who will be called "the Son of the Most High." That is quite an announcement. Mary, being a rational creature and therefore my kind of girl, asks a straightforward question, "How can this be, since I am a virgin?" Her curiosity is first a matter of simple biology. She knows how babies are made, and she doesn't have the experience necessary for this job. But on a deeper level her response is also a question of faith: "How can this be?" How can a human being be the means by which the "Son of the Most High" comes into the world? From my perspective, questions seem perfectly understandable in Mary's situation.

I admire Mary. I admire her ability first to face an angel, then to voice her questions, and finally to surrender herself to the angel's words and to God's working. As I have heard this story over the years, I have often wondered how many young girls Gabriel visited before he got to Mary and found someone willing to cooperate with what God wanted to do. I can imagine a weary and harried Gabriel looking at a long list of candidates' names, crossing them off one by one as young women breeze past him (unaware that God is trying to get their attention) or turn him down once he delivers the message: "Sorry, but you'll have to find yourself another girl, Gabe. This just isn't my kind of assignment." Is Mary the fourth young woman Gabriel visits that night? the fourteenth? the fortieth? The Bible doesn't tell us that Mary is the first, the only one, considered. We know simply that she is the one who says, "I am the Lord's servant. Let it be with me as you have said" (Luke 1:38, AP). All we know for sure is that Mary is the one who agrees—and that only after voicing her question and getting an answer.

Mary's question goes to the crux of our human struggle to understand the coming of God into the world. After all, how *can* it be? Even if we remove the virgin issue (which some do by pointing out that the word translated "virgin" here is translated as "young woman" in every other place it appears in the Bible), we still face the matter of Deity willingly accepting confinement in a human body. How can it be? We celebrate the fourth Sunday in Advent as the Sunday of mystery, illumination, incarnation. The idea of incarnation—God's putting Godself *in carne*, in flesh—is more than some people can accept. They can believe that God exists, that God is good, that God wills life for us and gives it. But incarnation? Well, that just doesn't make any kind of sense.

Those of us who struggle with this question or with any other idea about God can take comfort in knowing that Mary's questioning did not disqualify her from participating in what God was about to do. I have always asked questions myself, lots of them, and I know how disconcerting they can be to people. I remember stopping the assistant principal at my junior high school to talk in the hallway on numerous occasions. Sighing heavily during one of our difficult conversations, he said in exasperation, "Don't you ever get tired of asking questions?"

I answered with a question, of course: "But don't you always say that questions are the keys to knowledge?" He just walked away, shaking his head, unable to put up with any more. Most people prefer answers over questions.

Gabriel has more patience with Mary than the assistant principal had with me. Though that is not a surprise, it is worth noting. Gabriel stays with Mary as she questions. He doesn't say, "Sorry, no questions allowed," or leave to visit the next candidate on his list. Gabriel allows Mary to voice her questions, neither censuring her for lack of faith nor indicating that he found the questioning disconcerting or challenging. He stays. We don't know how long the angel is with Mary, but he does not leave until Mary reaches the point of being able to surrender herself to what God is asking. And she does not come to that point of surrender by rational means, convinced by the angel's arguments or by his quoting scripture at her. She simply says what is on her mind and heart. Gabriel responds to Mary by saying only, "The Holy Spirit will come upon you." Yeah, right. On this she is supposed to stake her reputation and her future? That would not be enough for me. But for Mary it is.

I have asked myself many times what makes Mary able to respond as she then does, saying, "Let it be with me according to your word." In part at least, I think she can make that response because Gabriel has listened to her honest questions without condemning her. This sets both questioning and listening in a new light. You and I have the opportunity to fulfill holy roles by honestly exploring our own questions and by being present, on God's behalf, with those who are going through times of questioning. By facing rather than burying or running from our questions, we may become able to say yes, finally, to what God asks of us. Sometimes we may be the one asking the questions, and sometimes we may be the messenger sent to be present on God's behalf with others as they explore their questions. In Mary's story, both roles are holy; God uses both. This part of Mary's experience suggests that voicing our questions in the presence of someone who allows us to speak honestly can move us toward being able to say yes to God.

LIVING WITH QUESTIONS

What do you suppose Mary was like in the moments, days, weeks, and months following her encounter with Gabriel? I wonder whether her serenity and surrender wavered as she considered what was happening. Becoming a parent is a life-changing event that forever alters one's perspective on the world, and I don't think anyone can appreciate that change before living through the process. I recall the day my daughter was born. People had talked about the rush of love that mothers feel, but when I looked at the helpless, vulnerable creature in my arms, this tiny person for whose care and nurture I would be responsible, all I could think was, *WHAT have I gotten myself into? Can I do this?* I wonder if Mary felt like that in the months between the angel's visit and Jesus' birth, as she sensed her body changing and the baby moving. And during those hours in the stable, during labor and after the birth, was she serene and submissive then? Or did she question her sanity, as well as God's goodness and sufficiency? And this baby for whom she had accepted responsibility was not an ordinary child; he was the Son of God and the Savior of the world! But I am getting ahead of the story.

After the angel's visit, both Mary and Joseph endure a great deal along the way to obeying God and parenting Jesus. Mary leaves home for several months, and Joseph considers divorcing Mary for adultery until a dream convinces him that he is in the middle of an unfolding miracle. But the angel's visit, Elizabeth's encouragement, and the dream that causes Joseph to stay with Mary were months behind the couple by the time they set out for Bethlehem. Perhaps the reality of those supernatural encounters has faded. Mary and Joseph are required to go to Bethlehem to be counted in the census even though Mary is heavy with child, and they are going in order to be taxed. This is not a pleasure trip. (Compare their attitude to the way we feel as we take our tax returns and checks to the post office on April 15.)

Joseph has to take Mary to the town of his birth. I wonder why they don't stay with Joseph's relatives rather than look for paid lodging. Is Joseph estranged from his family? Is Joseph an orphan? Has he been away for so many years that he no longer even knows how to find his relatives in the crowded city? Whatever the answers to those questions, no red carpet is rolled out, no one is waiting for them to arrive. Theirs isn't a joyous family homecoming like those we see in Christmas movies. When we begin to feel that something is wrong with us because our holidays are not free of loneliness, stress, disappointment, and unsatisfied yearnings, we do well to remember Mary and Joseph on that first Christmas. Unquestionably they have a difficult time, and it is going to get worse, ending with their fleeing to Egypt, fleeing for their lives. That eventuality is quite dramatic and far from peaceful and restful. But again, I am getting ahead of the story.

After the birth, Mary no doubt holds the baby and lets his little fingers curl around her own. Mothers and fathers do that. Considering that scene, I realize that God pays Mary and Joseph a great compliment by entrusting them with Eternal Hope. This baby is completely human and therefore vulnerable to disease, neglect, and their errors and insecurities as first-time parents. They probably don't understand the magnitude of what is going on and how Jesus' life will unfold any more than other parents can comprehend the future of their newborn children. Luke 2:33 describes Mary and Joseph as "amazed at what was being said about" Jesus. Like them, most of the time, we don't step back to see the bigger picture, and when we try, we often see no pattern, nothing to reassure us that events are unfolding according to any plan we can discern.

When we consider the vulnerability of that tiny boy Jesus in the hands of an inexperienced couple far from home, the question comes to mind again: *How can this be? How could God take the risk of becoming a human baby?* The proposition seems entirely too dangerous, from a purely operational perspective. Too many things could go wrong with entrusting the hope of salvation to fallible folks like Mary and Joseph.

Yet except for their ending up sleeping in a stable, everything seems all right on the night of Jesus' birth, in spite of the people involved. A remarkable fact about the Christmas events is that God works through not simply ordinary people but through those who are despised and dismissed—widows, women who can't get pregnant, babies born to poor families in obscure places. Mary isn't a nice middle-class girl, and she and Joseph don't check into a Holiday Inn or a Hilton. They are poor. And another thing: In a culture where women were property and men held most of the power, the "speaking parts" in the Christmas drama go to women. Up to this point the men are, in fact, curiously silent (especially Zechariah, who is silenced for months). Conventional wisdom held that God moved through kings, wars, armies, plagues, through stunning miracles like rolling back seas and stopping the sun—not through babies and women. These are not among the usual cast of characters in epics. In Hebrew scripture, most of those God uses seem certain of their tasks and message. They don't ask questions; they answer them. They thunder, "Hear the word of the LORD" and "Thus saith the LORD," and similar intimidating phrases. Not the questioners in the Christmas story. They don't always seem to know that they are in the middle of God's acts, and they use questionable methods. Tamar and Rahab use outright trickery and lies; Ruth and Naomi cleverly use custom to snare Boaz. Elizabeth secludes herself in her home. Mary questions an angel (and gets away with it, though, curiously, Zechariah does not). These are not arrogant, self-assured, seasoned leaders.

One lesson I draw from Mary's questioning is that we have permission to ask questions, to be less than sure, to engage God and God's messengers when we have questions, when obedience does not come automatically. That knowledge comforts me, because I too have questions. I admit that I envy those who seem certain of everything about their faith. I am not always sure about everything in mine. I know from many conversations that I am not the only one either. Somewhere along the way in growing up, many of us have lost some of our certainty about God and other truths. Some of us have left behind the ability to embrace easily truths that don't make sense to us rationally. And along with this loss, we have also lost our ability to accept faith's contradictions and ambiguities.

AMBIGUITIES OF FAITH

My niece once pressed her mother to pray with her for the resurrection of their cat after the pet met with an unfortunate accident. When the animal was not brought back to life, I feared my niece's faith would be shaken. There was no need for alarm or explanation. She simply accepted that sometimes resurrection happens, and sometimes it does not. It was not a problem for her. But many of us more sophisticated believers have difficulty with ambiguous situations as well as what seem to be inconsistencies in the faith and in the way God works. We may struggle in worship, unable to join in reciting creeds whose tenets we do not fully accept, unable to sing hymns whose theology sticks in our throats. And since believing is an all-or-nothing proposition for many people, those with questions may keep quiet about them in order not to alarm anyone. (Keeping quiet almost guarantees, of course, that answers will come much more slowly than when we ask for help or information, but at least folks won't be upset.)

Belief and doubt are two sides of a single question about finding meaning and direction in life. Though the question is ancient, we modern people seem no closer to finding answers than earlier seekers. John Irving's wonderful book *A Prayer for Owen Meany* follows the life of an honest searcher after personal faith. Nearly everyone in the book, in fact, wrestles in some way with issues of belief. Owen, the title character, remarkable in many ways, resolutely believes that God has chosen him for a specific and unusual role. Others in the story (including the narrator, Owen's best friend) walk tortured paths trying to work out their questions about what the church teaches and even about whether God exists. Their modern minds seem to know almost too much to allow belief in miracles, but still they struggle to make sense of how God is active in them and in the world. Those who do believe in the greatest miracle of the story are presented as the most weird, even crazy. Believing does not make Owen's life easy, and it does not make our lives easy, any more than it does Mary's. Both belief and doubt stir up our lives. The Christians in *A Prayer for Owen Meany* face as many challenges as the nonbelievers, and they voice as many questions—sometimes the same questions.

The concept of the Incarnation is one that causes struggle for many of us. How can Christ be simultaneously completely God and completely human? The Bible says not just that God took on flesh but that God *became* flesh. As I think of Mary "pondering all these things in her heart," I see her sitting mute before the mystery of the Incarnation. It is impossible to explain to anyone's rational satisfaction. How can Jesus be both human and divine? One law of physics that we all know intuitively is that two objects cannot occupy the same space at the same time. (Even if we've never taken a physics course, we say, "Something is going to have to come out before this can go in" as we try to stuff one more garment into the suitcase.) When we try to think of Jesus as simultaneously fully human and fully divine, our human minds start sputtering. It doesn't sound possible. But then I remember that we may understand parts of some processes and still be unable to explain the whole. Take genetics, for example. Although we know about dominant and recessive genes and can produce charts about probabilities and percentages, we can't explain why some sons look like carbon copies of their fathers while others look like masculine versions of their mothers, why some daughters look like miniatures of their mothers and others like feminine versions of their fathers. If we can't explain such common occurrences even with all the information we have gathered, how can we hope to grasp how Jesus is "very God of very God"? Ultimately we cannot grasp this concept and many other truths with our rational minds, because reason and intellect can never get us where we want to go regarding belief. But we continue to wish they could.

Some of us struggle for certainty, and some add to that spiritual load by also worrying about the fact that we are struggling. Yet when we hesitate to voice our questions, even to those closest to us, the spinning logic wheels in our mind can distract us from experiencing the reality of God. We produce questions that are impossible to answer. Some people struggle so intensely that they become disillusioned with faith; some become estranged from God and organized religion and leave the church. Others may float in a kind of malaise within the church—less than happy, less than faithful, feeling less than loved by God and yet unable to leave the faith behind completely. But it is possible to face our questions and doubts and to wrestle with them until we exhaust our rational powers and are able to move beyond their limits.

I take comfort in remembering that the church struggled to come to agreement about a number of faith concepts—some for centuries, and some are still under discussion. Paul and the disciples differed over whether new believers had to become Jews to be welcomed into the church. Believers argued for centuries about Jesus' nature and the sense in which he was God's Son. As late as the eighth century, a bishop named Felix was kicked out of office for espousing adoptionism, one belief about Jesus' role as God's Son. Belief and acceptance are not automatic or easy. So I admire Mary in her ability to accept what God was doing, even without a rational answer to satisfy her question. She accepted the mystery of God's coming, apart from understanding it.

Living with mystery is not the same thing as believing in magic. In the arena of literature and film, "willing suspension of disbelief" describes the process by which we admit that something cannot possibly happen but put aside that "knowledge" in order to enjoy a story where humans fly, godmothers grant wishes, or people travel through time. We "suspend" our disbelief—our knowledge that parts of the story do not make sense—in order to enter into the story. This is not the process involved in coming to faith. We do not have to put aside our rationality or put questions out of our minds, as if they never arose.

French theologian Paul Ricoeur writes about a concept that I find helpful, a concept that is translated "second naiveté." (What follows is my understanding of Ricoeur's thought and certainly is not intended as a scholarly treatment of the topic.) He discusses the human need to reconcile belief with rationality. Some people move through questioning, disillusionment, attempts at rational analysis of faith, even estrangement from God and organized religion. After all this, they may finally decide that some tenets of faith are unexplainable, but they come to a place of affirming them again anyway—a place of "second naiveté" where they accept these truths on faith, apart from rational certainty and in spite of doubts. Like my niece's attitude about resurrection and lack thereof, we may decide that we will not wrestle with ambiguities and contradictions. We come to see that some concepts—like the Incarnation—can never be proven or explained. But we decide to embrace them anyway as a part of the great Mystery that is God, surrendering our need for proof and explanation, surrendering ourselves to God's ways, as Mary did.

Each year when the Christmas movie *Miracle on 34th Street* airs, I am reminded of our twin needs to question and to believe. In that movie, a sophisticated woman and her child each meet and come to care for a man who claims to be Kris Kringle—Santa Claus. The movie follows their experiences. Though their questions are handled in a somewhat lighthearted way and are not about Christian faith, the dynamic is similar to raising questions within our faith. The woman decides finally that not to believe contradicts what her heart has learned. Many of us think we are too sophisticated for belief. We are grown-ups, after all, and we have moved beyond childish acceptance of what clearly does not make sense. But God offers us anew in each Advent season the opportunity to claim our faith, as with Mary we voice our questions and acknowledge our doubts. We can decide that it will never make sense rationally—and choose to believe anyway.

The consequences of our choosing to believe are both far-reaching and intimately personal. When we accept the wonder of God's taking on flesh and coming to us in Christ, our view of these bodies of flesh is forever different. Christ, though he was God, was "born in human likeness." His taking on our humanness makes humanness holy in a way it was not before. The refrain of the faithful can then become not "this despised body" but "this blessed body." We do not have to hate our humanness: fat thighs, limp hair, sore muscles, crooked noses—these too are the objects of God's blessing and the locus of God's activity. Greek dualism saw the world in terms of good/bad, body/spirit, solid/liquid, and other opposites. (We see this influence reflected in much of the apostle Paul's reasoning and in his theology.) Bodies were bad and spiritual selves were good, and the two opposed each other. But because Christ became completely human, bad flesh versus good spirit becomes a false dichotomy. Just as we now know that "solid" metals become liquid at high temperatures and cancel the solid/liquid opposite we once called true, Christ's becoming flesh wipes out the idea that fleshly humanness is bad while only spirit can be good. In Jesus Christ we see what God wants us to be and how God wants us to live; Jesus the Christ is human, whole, and very good. This new vision of and appreciation for our humanity are gifts of the Incarnation.

Jesus told Philip that he came not just to tell us what God is like but to show us what God is like (see John 14:8-9). Jesus came in order to embody goodness and fullness of life. Knowing us, God knows that we sensory humans need to see, to hear, to feel, to touch. Writer Leith Anderson tells a story about American missionaries who went to the Philippines. Assessing the situation of the poor in Manila, these missionaries went to live on—not near, but *on*—a garbage dump in Manila, where the poor people were already living. The missionaries intended not to tell the people about God's love but to show them that love. What they did was remarkable, but it is nothing compared to what God did in Christ. Christ left behind equality with God to live among us. That is Advent's message.

When we compare God's act to our own actions (as we humans always do, centered as we are in the physical world), it seems impossible that God would willingly accept the limitations and dangers of living in a mortal body. With Mary we ask, "How can this be . . . ?" This question and all our other questions can serve to remind us that Christmas is about not what our head knows but what our heart knows. Every Christmas is an invitation to surrender to that heart knowledge—or to as much of it as we can. Mary and Joseph listen to the messages of the angels and of the shepherds and look deep into their dreams, but they do not understand all at once what they hear and see. Nevertheless they surrender to it. They "live into" its meaning over time. When Jesus is presented at the temple as an infant, Mary and Joseph are "amazed" at Simeon's words. They do not understand the twelve-year-old Jesus' words about being "about my Father's business." The two do not fully comprehend what God is doing in Jesus, even after angel visits, God-given dreams, and Jesus' own statements.

Jesus' parents are not the only ones who do not grasp all the truth of who he is. John the Baptist, named from his birth as a prophet who is to prepare the way for the Messiah, baptizes Jesus at the beginning of Jesus' ministry. But John still is not completely sure about Jesus' identity and about the sense in which Jesus represents God. At one point John sends his disciples to ask Jesus, "Are you the one who is to come, or are we to wait for another?" (Matt. 11:3). When we ask questions about Jesus, we are in good company. Nevertheless people often equate questioning with denouncing faith, and calling someone a "Doubting Thomas" (or Thomasina) is not a compliment.

It is human to ask for assurances (remember Tamar's and Zechariah's questions?), but God seldom answers in the form we request. I notice that over and over when people question Jesus about theology and rules, he turns the discussion away from rules and proofs and back to relationship. God offers not theological discussions or rational proofs but relationship. Jesus' question to the disciples, "Who do people say that the Son of Man is?" (Matt. 16:13) is a theological question. But he moves immediately to another question, "Who do you say that I am?" (Matt. 16:15). That is a relationship question. Jesus shows us again and again that God always acts in our lives to draw us into relationship. When Simon Peter answers Jesus, "You are the Messiah," Jesus points out that this insight is not something Peter has come to through his own wisdom, saying, "Flesh and blood has not revealed this to you." When Mary questions, the angel tells her, "The Holy Spirit will come . . . ," reminding her that flesh and blood do not have to accomplish this miraculous feat or figure out God's purpose. God responds to our questions—maybe not with information to satisfy our minds, but God responds. As Christ does with Thomas, God responds to our questions by drawing closer to us and reaching out to us.

THE VALUE OF QUESTIONING

Facing our questions and our doubts can lead us to discover truth. In discussing with a friend a matter I had been praying about, I admitted that even as I had asked God to do something, I did not really believe God would do it. I told my friend that this realization made me hesitate even to pray, since it seemed arrogant or disrespectful or somehow negative to ask when I did not think it likely that God would act. My friend replied, "I think we are supposed to come to God with the faith we do have, not the faith we don't have. And God accepts that." Thinking about his words, I would now add, "And God is pleased with that." It is our approaching as much as the amount and content of our faith that pleases God, because what God desires is not intellectual assent from us but relationship with us. Reason and intellect will never get us where we need to go. Miracles of any sort—babies for the barren, belief for the skeptic, transformation of a "heart of stone" into a "heart of flesh"—are counterrational. Always have been, always will be. Yet Mary surrenders herself to irrational truth and cooperates in what God already is doing. It always comes back to that kind of surrender.

Mary and Joseph go to Bethlehem. That is significant, but it is not all that significant. Many others do the same. What is eternally significant is that God comes to Bethlehem, and God takes on a body. We may not feel at home with all we hear at Christmas, but God will still come to us. Every year, God says, "I'll be home for Christmas." And our welcome is what God wants.

We don't have to understand what God is doing in order to participate in it or to know that it is real. If complete understanding were necessary in order to know that something is real, in order to use it, few of us could use telephones or computers or electricity because few of us understand those technologies. But we can accept them as gifts and benefit from their presence in our lives without understanding them.

God doesn't want us as a business partner, as a distant relative, even as a close friend. God wants to live with each one of us, as one of us. That is the miracle of Christmas. God takes on flesh. It sounds impossible. Do we choose to believe it anyway? The angel closed the conversation with Mary by reminding her who is behind it all: "For nothing will be impossible with God." God's coming doesn't depend on us, on the depth or steadiness of our believing. This miracle depends on God, whom we cannot understand or contain, who reaches out to us at Christmas and every day of our lives. As Mary shows us, finding ourselves slightly puzzled and in awe before this mystery is a faithful response.

REFLECTION PAGES

DAY 1 REFLECTION

Read Luke 1:26-38.

Reflect.

The angel greeted Mary as "favored one" and said, "The Lord is with you." Why do you think Mary found that greeting perplexing?

Mary's question to the angel seemed like a simple request for information. Do you think it was something more? What do you think she needed at that moment?

Who has stayed with you in your times of questioning? Did you see your companion(s) as God's messenger(s) at the time?

For what questions would you like answers today?

Think of someone you know who is at the edge of responding to an invitation from God. How can you be with that person on God's behalf?

_____

_____

_____

_____

_____

_____

Rest.

Listen as God says to you, "I am with you." Consider what this means for you today.

Pray a breath prayer.

For a breath prayer until your next time of reflection, consider praying, "O God, I give you my questions."

DAY 2 REFLECTION

Read Luke 1:46-55.

Reflect.

This passage is known as "Mary's Song." Imagine what sort of melody might accompany these words. What tempo and mood would fit them? Why?

_____

_____

_____

_____

_____

_____

_____

Mary says, "All generations will call me blessed." In what sense do you see Mary as blessed? In what ways do you see her as more challenged than blessed?

Some of Mary's words say that God deposes the mighty from their thrones and sends the rich away empty. How might such changes be a sign of coming salvation?

If you were writing a song today about what God has done in your life, what events and relationships would you include ? Why?

Rest.
Sit in God's presence and reflect on how future generations will consider you blessed. How has God acted through you and in your life?

Pray a breath prayer.
For a breath prayer until your next time of reflection, consider praying, "God of joy, come into the world through me."

DAY 3 REFLECTION

Read Psalm 146.

Reflect.
Identify the traits of God mentioned here that are also mentioned in Mary's song in Luke 1.

Which of God's traits and actions move you to praise?

Where do you see oppressed people in need of God's help as Christmas approaches? What will they need after Christmas?

What Christmas carols remind you that Jesus' coming is meant to change the world and the way we do things?

_____
_____
_____
_____
_____
_____
_____
_____
_____
_____
_____
_____
_____
_____
_____
_____
_____
_____
_____
_____
_____
_____

Rest.

Consider how God executes judgment, feeds the hungry, sets prisoners free, gives sight to the blind, and befriends the stranger and the fatherless today. Through whom does God do these things? Hold these people before God and ask that they be blessed and encouraged.

Pray a breath prayer.

For a breath prayer until your next time of reflection, consider praying, "God of freedom, I praise you."

DAY 4 REFLECTION

Read 1 Corinthians 2:7-16.

Reflect.

What parts of "God's wisdom" are hard for you to understand?

_____
_____
_____
_____

Why do you think some truths about God are still mystery to us? Why is mystery a part of our faith?

_____
_____
_____
_____

Which of your human traits sometimes get in your way as you try to understand and follow God?

_____
_____

What have you learned about God that you know in your heart is true but you cannot explain rationally? Are you comfortable with truths you cannot explain?

_____
_____
_____
_____
_____
_____

Rest.

Rest in the presence of Mystery. Without asking for understanding, welcome God. Acknowledge that you cannot understand, and simply sit with God in silence.

Pray a breath prayer.

For a breath prayer until your next time of reflection, consider praying, "God of Mystery, welcome."

Day 5 Reflection

Read John 20:24-28.

Reflect.

What have you been taught about "Doubting Thomas"?

_____
_____
_____
_____

How do you feel about Thomas after reading this passage? What praiseworthy traits do you see in him?

_____
_____
_____

Imagine Christ standing before Thomas and extending his hands so Thomas can touch them. What expression is on Thomas's face? What expression is on Christ's face?

What does it mean to you that Christ reaches out to this one who needs reassurance, this one who struggles to believe?

_____

_____

_____

_____

_____

_____

_____

_____

_____

_____

Rest.
Bring your doubts, questions, and fears. As you hold them out to God, imagine Christ drawing near to you. Say whatever you need to say. Look at his face. Listen to what he says to you. Stay with Christ as long as you wish.

Pray a breath prayer.
For a breath prayer until your next time of reflection, consider praying, "Loving Christ, stay close to me."

CHAPTER 5

SHARING THE LIGHT: WHERE IS THE ONE?

Christ has no hands but ours, no eyes but ours, . . . to reach out to a hurting world.

—Teresa of Avila

The last question of Advent comes not at Christmas but afterward and is asked not by an individual but by a group. The Magi, sages from the East who come seeking the Christ Child, ask this question. These men are astrologers—stargazers who read the sky for clues about events on earth—and they have seen a special star. They believe that the unusual star (some speculate not just a single star but an unusual conjunction of heavenly bodies that produces an especially bright light) marks the birth of a special child destined to be a king. The Magi come asking, "Where is the child who has been born king of the Jews?" Tradition has it that there were three Magi, probably because the Bible account names three gifts (gold, frankincense, and myrrh). The names used for these Magi are Caspar, Melchior, and Balthasar, and tradition also says that they are of three different ethnic groups, signifying that Christ comes not just for one nation but for all people. In fact, that is what we celebrate in January at Epiphany: Jesus Christ as the Light of the world. We celebrate Christ as Light to the whole world, not as the Light to one small group in the world.

Many Christians mark Epiphany in only cursory ways, as if everything about Christmas ends at midnight on December 25. We do seem in a hurry sometimes to put away Christmas. One friend of mine undecorates and usually has all the Christmas things in the attic by mid-afternoon on December 26, explaining, "When it's over, it's over." Most of us stop playing Christmas music, too, as if the songs are inappropriate at any other time of year. I leave my Christmas music discs in the CD player well into the new year, and those who visit my home usually comment when they hear a Christmas song playing. (Working on this book gave me a good reason to play the Christmas CDs well into the summer, which really elicited comments. I just kept saying it was "for atmosphere" while I worked on this book manuscript.)

Commentators have said we seem in a hurry after Christmas to box up once again our patience, our tolerance, our generosity and put them back in the attic, as if we can sustain good behavior for a few weeks but wouldn't want to risk making it a way of life. We may also put away our willingness to give a bit more, to be more forgiving, even to be more patient in traffic as we often are during the holidays. Perhaps we even box up our desire to hope and our openness to miracles and mystery, as if the messages of the Christmas stories can't quite survive the rigors of real life the rest of the year. The Magi call us to continue our observance of Christ's coming after December is over.

In all likelihood, the Magi traveled in a caravan with a larger group of people, for protection. (This probability allows us to add camels to our Nativity scenes, since caravans used camels in crossing the desert.) Maybe only three people joined a merchant caravan for convenience as they followed the star, but perhaps there were many who came to find Jesus. In any case, we include the story of the Magi's journey in our Christmas pageants and place them in our crèche scenes, even if doing so takes a little liberty with the time line. (Jesus is a young child according to the Magi account, so the three probably did not arrive at the stable.)

In fact, during the Christmas season, we don't usually hear all that scripture includes about the events that followed Jesus' birth. For instance, most of us are not as familiar with the stories of Anna and Simeon as we are with the stories of the angels and shepherds. Yet Anna and Simeon have the honor of recognizing Jesus as the Messiah and proclaiming who he is when others seem not to be noticing him. They appear in the story of Jesus' dedication in the temple at Jerusalem.

Anna is an elderly woman who spends all her time praying and praising God. At age eighty-four, she has been a widow for many years and never leaves the temple. Simeon is "righteous and devout, looking forward to the consolation of Israel" (Luke 2:25). Luke records that "the Holy Spirit rested on" Simeon. The Holy Spirit had revealed to Simeon that he would not die until he had seen the Lord's Messiah (Luke 2:25-26). On the day that Mary and Joseph bring Jesus in, Simeon, "guided by the Spirit," shows up, too. On seeing the child, Simeon does something unusual for a man of those times. Children were women's concern, and men had little to do with them, especially children outside their families. But Simeon takes in his arms this baby whom he does not know.

Imagine this scene as a movie and listen to the soundtrack as Simeon sees the baby and takes him in his arms. The volume of the background music gradually increases as Simeon praises God's compassion and gives thanks for having been allowed to see the Messiah. Then, as he proclaims Jesus to be God's salvation for Israel, the music swells into a joyous crescendo. Then the music begins to change, modulating to a minor key, one that sounds foreboding, as Simeon says that this child will be "a light for revelation to the Gentiles" (Luke 2:32), who are foreigners, not God's people. Perhaps the music here begins to mirror sounds associated with "the East," hinting of the visitors yet to come. Finally Simeon turns to Mary only, saying that this baby "is destined for the falling and rising of many in Israel and to be a sign that will be opposed" (Luke 2:34). Here the music slows, as Simeon's next words foreshadow sorrow during what has been a celebration. He says to Mary, "And a sword will pierce your own soul too" (Luke 2:35). Mary's mother heart must surely think, *My soul too? What is he saying? Who else's soul is going to be pierced? Is he saying that my son will suffer pain and unhappiness, that his soul will be pierced?* And the music ends with an unresolved chord hanging in the air, leaving us to wonder about Simeon's meaning and the conclusion of this baby's story.

FACING THE WORLD'S EVIL

Mary and Joseph are "amazed" at Simeon's words. The angels had told them that this child would be a savior, but this wise and holy old man says Jesus will cause great trouble for many in Israel. Simeon seems to say that this baby will play a powerful role politically. Even more shocking, the child will influence Gentiles as well as Jews. This prediction goes beyond what the angel said, what Elizabeth said, what Joseph knew from his dreams. Good Jews had nothing to do with Gentiles. The tone of this encounter is very different from the joy of the angels singing to the shepherds or from Mary's hymn of praise for the "great things" God has done for her. Perhaps this ominous feeling explains why we do not dwell on Simeon's words about Mary's soul being pierced or on the rest of the Magi's story. We want Christmas to be a joyful time, and we leave no place for discussions of trouble and pierced souls. So we don't look too closely at this part of the story.

And it gets worse. The story of the Magi, this chapter's questioners, culminates in the darkest scene of the Christmas story, in an episode we don't want to explore with our children. We don't even want to explore it ourselves. The Magi come looking for a future king, and they begin looking where they expect to find such a person: in the royal household. They go to Herod, the governor of Galilee, asking, "Where is the child who has been born king of the Jews?" Sensing a possible rival, Herod "was frightened, and all Jerusalem with him" (Matt. 2:3). This statement should tell us something about Herod's nature, methods, and reputation. When he becomes upset, the entire city is upset. People fear not what Herod knows but what he will do. After hearing the Magi's account of the reason for their journey, Herod summons and questions his own diviners regarding prophecies about the birth of a child who will become "king of the Jews." The diviners tell him that according to the prophet Micah (Mic. 5:2), the child will come from Bethlehem. Then Herod calls the Magi to him "secretly" and finds out from them exactly when the star appeared. He asks them to let him know when they find the future king so he may go and pay homage too. In reality, of course, Herod wants to eliminate, not worship, this potential rival. He will try to eliminate any challenger. After meeting with Herod, the Gentile visitors go on to Bethlehem, where they find Jesus, the "child." They present their gifts, and "having been warned in a dream not to return to Herod" (Matt. 2:12), they slip away and go home without telling Herod about finding Jesus. When Herod discovers what the Magi have done, he is "infuriated." But he will not be thwarted in finding this rival princeling. In his fury, he issues a horrifying order: Go and kill all the children two years old and younger in and around Bethlehem. The assassins head for Bethlehem to do as Herod commanded.

This slaughter gives us a glimpse of horrible evil. It is one of the most disturbing atrocities recorded in the Bible. Some churches commemorate this event as Holy Innocents' Day, but many of us shrink from talking or even thinking about it. The slaughter of the innocents contradicts the warm, fuzzy feelings that characterize most of our Christmas traditions, making us sad and uneasy. In facing this event, we face questions that we don't want to ask or try to answer.

Why didn't God protect the innocents? That is a difficult question, one that we continue to ask when modern innocents die. We asked it after the bombing of the Murrah Federal Building in Oklahoma City in 1995, haunted by the image of the firefighter carrying a mortally wounded toddler from the wreckage. Why didn't God step in and at least shield little Baylee and the others like her who were in that day-care center? We ask it when we hear stories of famine in faraway places or of children being used as soldiers. We asked it in horror after the destruction of the World Trade Center in New York City. As the plane exploded through the second tower, people around the world wept at the loss of human life. I have imagined a scene symbolic of the tragedy: Father Mychal Judge, chaplain to firefighters, kneeling to administer last rites to an injured rescuer. Removing his hard hat in that holy moment, the priest reportedly was mortally wounded by falling debris. Why must the innocent suffer? We still ask that question, and always we ask it from the midst of pain.

Though we cannot answer that question, the story of the slaughtered innocents reminds us of an important truth: Jesus comes into this world as it actually is, not as we might wish it to be. A harsh reality of the message of salvation is that we truly *need* salvation. Evil is real, and the ways of this world can and do crush life. God's way unsettles the entrenched powers of the world, and they resist. Remember Mary's song?

> [God] has scattered the proud in the thoughts of their hearts.
> He has brought down the powerful from their thrones,
>   and lifted up the lowly;
> he has filled the hungry with good things,
>   and sent the rich away empty.
>
> —Luke 1:51-53

Anyone powerful and rich would feel threatened by a world like the one Mary proclaims. The "good news of great joy" the angels proclaim does not mean that the world will be suddenly, magically different. Jesus is eventually killed, too, just as the children of Bethlehem are. Anna and Simeon recognize the Messiah, but do they recognize how his message will shake the world? Simeon, at least, indicates that Jesus' life and Mary's will not be easy when he mentions the sword that will pierce Mary's soul. Looking forward to Jesus' trial and crucifixion, we know that Simeon is heartbreakingly right.

The tough, ugly truth of this story reminds us that the world's powerful oppose the coming of the new world of God's reign. When change threatens to take power from the powerful, they seek to stop it, cancel it out, obliterate it, even if innocents have to die in the process. And as incredible as it sounds, we may adjust ourselves to such horrors without realizing what we are accepting. When civilians are killed in war along the way to reaching a military objective, their deaths are called "collateral damage." Homes are bombed when air bases are the targets; hospitals are destroyed instead of factories. Collateral damage. It is regrettable, but some events like this are inevitable. It can't be helped. "War is hell," as we all have heard and know.

But we don't want to face life's harsh realities as we think about children. When children are born, we want to believe they will all grow up healthy and happy. We don't want to know that this child will become an addict, that child will die of an illness in childhood, this one will never really find a purpose and will drift through life, that child over there will be consumed by greed and become ruthless and cruel in the push to get ahead, and this one will be abused. We don't want to hear about the evil that is part of life. Yet we need the Light of the world in exactly those dark places. The world needs the message of wholeness that Christ proclaimed, and we all need the healing that is possible with God. We need to know Emmanuel—that God is with us—and the world's people need someone to introduce them to Emmanuel.

We who are believers say that Christ is real and alive and acting in the world. That is not just good news; it is great news. People want to believe and need to hear, over and over, the message of God's active and powerful good will. Perhaps it is appropriate that a group of people (the Magi) ask, "Where is the child who has been born king of the Jews?" The fact that a group rather than an individual presents this question suggests that this is the world's basic question, asked in myriad ways: "Where is the Promised One, the One who will save and heal?" In many ways people come to us as individuals and come into our churches, asking in effect, "Where is the one who has been born king of the Jews?" Where is the new way of life that I have heard about? Where is the Christ? Some of these seekers have journeyed a long time, looking for Christ in many places but not finding him, never being shown Christ by one of his followers. Some of them are deeply weary, their "hearts . . . bowed down with hard labor," as the psalm says (Ps. 107:12). They need healing and hope and the peace of God.

L I V I N G   L I G H T S

According to the prophecies, Christ will bring peace and Christ is our peace. The peace that Christ brings is much wider and deeper than the absence of war. The peace that Christ brings is the *shalom* depicted in Hebrew scripture—a world where the hungry are fed, where people grow toward wholeness, where the entire created order is cared for, where all oppression ends, where all of God's children receive God's abundance with thankful hearts because they recognize its source. The prophet Jeremiah pictures God's desire for shalom, saying, "I know the plans I have for you, says the Lord, plans for your welfare and not for harm, to give you a future with hope" (Jer. 29:11). God wants this abundant life for us, the abundant life Jesus came to give. Yet when we place this vision alongside the harsh realities of life, we may almost despair of the world's ever being what God desires. Christmas makes its promises, but the world doesn't seem much different this year than last or the year before that or the year before that. Kids shoot their classmates; disgruntled employees attack coworkers; bombers kill children in shopping malls; refugees stream out of war-torn countries. "Where is the Christ? Where is Peace?" the crowd asks. "Where is the One born to be our Savior?"

We hear people say about something that sounds good, "I'll believe it when I see it." We who know Christ have the opportunity to let others "see it," to show them Christ. We can embody for the world the answer to the question, "Where is the One born to save us?" As Paul tells the Corinthians, "You are the body of Christ and individually members of it" (1 Cor. 12:27). As the Epistle to the Galatians puts it, "It is no longer I who live, but it is Christ who lives in me" (Gal. 2:20). And in Colossians, "Christ is all and in all" (Col. 3:11). You and I have the privilege of continuing the Incarnation. In the Eastern Orthodox tradition, Mary the mother of Jesus is called *theotokos*, which is literally translated "God-bearer." Mary bore Christ into the world, and all those who share in the life that Christ gives can also become "God-bearers" in the world. People come to the church expecting to hear about God and find God, just as they come into a restaurant expecting to find food. Do they see God in us? Do they encounter Love and realize its power through their interactions with us?

I know one woman who would say that she did experience Love in her encounter with Christians. I'll call her Jayne. Needing help, Jayne came to the downtown church where I was a member. With no car, no job and six children—ranging in age from eighteen months to ten years—she was in need; her family was in need. Though Jayne had a husband, his problems kept him from reliably caring for the family. Jayne became a member of the Sunday school class I attended, and we became friends. Over time, many of us in the class spent time in her home, and Jayne spent time in ours. Her children sat on our laps and played games with us and with our children. More than money, she needed friendship, support, and people to help her have hope. Eventually she took a part-time job in our children's department.

Although I moved away from that town, I thought of Jayne often over the years, and I continued to pray for her and her family. Then, literally as I was working on this chapter, I received a letter from Jayne. I was amazed and pleased to hear how her situation has changed. After Jayne's troubled marriage ended, someone introduced her to a man on the church staff who was also a single parent. Eventually the two married. Jayne became the happy mother of a blended family and has ten grandchildren. All along the way, that church and its people have been a part of God's work in her life. The changes did not happen overnight, to be sure. More than twenty years have passed since she first walked into that church. But the difficulties and fear that limited her and her children lost their power when confronted by steady love. How does God transform the world? One heart at a time, one person at a time, one family at a time. We don't have to confront the world's Herods, matching power with power, to confound the forces of death and evil. As the Christmas carol says, "How silently, how silently, the wondrous gift is given." God slips quietly into the world, stealthily, waiting to overturn strongholds.

You may say to yourself, *I am not the sort of person God would choose to help change the world.* I imagine that's exactly what Mary thought. And those shepherds near Bethlehem, do they match our image of message-bearers from God? Shepherds were fringe people, at best. When Jesus spoke of himself as a shepherd, he had to put "good" in front of "shepherd" to be sure his hearers would envision someone other than the more usual sort of shepherd. Shepherds probably would not be anyone's messengers of choice, but Luke describes the shepherds as the first to publicly proclaim the "good news of great joy." God chooses and uses unlikely people. An angel did not visit the "important" people of the time like Quirinius or Herod. The angel came to Zechariah, described by writer John Indermark as "a minor temple official never heard from again," and to Mary, a peasant girl of no particular note. The forerunner of Jesus was a weird prophet named John who dressed in scratchy camel's hair and lived as a hermit, subsisting on bugs and wild honey. These folks were not from the upper echelons of their society. We see that God repeatedly turns the usual power system on its ear, ignoring the biggies and using obscure people like Tamar, Rahab, Ruth, and John—people whose availability and willingness to surrender to an uncertain future qualify them as instruments of God.

The season of Epiphany proclaims the truth that Christ comes to all people and will come to our neighborhoods, our towns, our workplaces if we are willing to allow the love of God to be incarnate in us. Every situation that calls for healing and hope offers us the privilege and the responsibility of representing and re-presenting Christ. Where is the Savior? Where is Christ? Take a look in a mirror. Are you willing to say, "Right here"? That sounds arrogant, doesn't it? But where else will God be made real and visible if not in us who say we are Christians?

I am ashamed to say that sometimes we see love—and God is love—more clearly in those who claim no faith than in those of us who do. I became particularly aware of this paradox when our Sunday school class curriculum directed us to reflect on where we had seen God. At the time I lived in a middle-class neighborhood where most of us owned our homes, but there were a few renters, whom we held in some disdain. Among them was one family who were not the sort of folks we were accustomed to having as neighbors. The man drove a noisy pickup truck that was perpetually primer gray and on which he worked nearly every weekend. Although the man was clean and kept his hair combed, he came outside wearing no shirt, and a cigarette constantly dangled from his lips or fingers. Some of my neighbors called them *rednecks*, a word some Southerners use to sum up a host of characteristics that we hope our families have left behind permanently. But they were a loving family. The father often played outside with his kids— riding bikes, shooting baskets, just watching over them.

Also on our street was a group home for retarded men. I saw the men frequently, and one of them, David, sometimes helped me bring in the groceries or accompanied me as I walked my dog. David was talkative and outgoing, telling me about his latest kite or toy as we walked. Another of the men, whom I'll call Kenny, older than David, was quite shy and seldom spoke. If David were present, Kenny let him to do the talking. One weekend, the one before that Sunday school class when we talked about seeing God, I was out walking the dog when Kenny was outside. I stopped to engage him in conversation. He was loading baseball equipment into the car, and I was sure I could get him to talk about going to the park, which I knew he enjoyed. But he responded warily, only in monosyllables. Then, as he looked over my shoulder, I saw his eyes light up. I turned to see that my truck-driving neighbor was pulling into the drive. Kenny stepped past me and hurried over, a smile transforming his face. When our neighbor got out of the car, Kenny enveloped him in a warm hug, which was heartily returned. The man gave Kenny a high five, calling him by name and saying, "How's it going, man?" It was clear that this man disdained by his neighbors had built a warm and accepting relationship with the shy man who could not quite trust me. Who had been embodying the love of God for Kenny? Neither I nor my uncomfortable neighbors could claim that distinction. In the embrace between Kenny and our neighbor, I saw Christ's love. God will reach into the world. That is God's nature. Who will be available?

When my friend Althea was going through seminary, she worked as a hospital chaplain under the guidance of an experienced clergyperson. By observing and doing, she would learn how to walk "through the waters" (Isa. 43:2) with those in crisis. Althea told me that each time before she went into a hospital room, she paused in the hallway, looked down at her sneakers, took a deep breath, and said to herself, "Okay, Althea, go in there and be God to these people. Be God to them." At first I thought her words and attitude were almost blasphemous. But the more I thought about them, the more clear it became to me that she had it exactly right. If people are to experience the love, patience, acceptance, and healing that is God, we have to embody those qualities. If people are going to experience God, it will have to happen through human instruments like us. As I said before, we are sensate creatures. We cannot help being shaped and influenced by what we see, hear, smell, feel, and taste. If people are to know the fragrance of mercy, the warmth of being included and welcomed, the sweetness of feeling forgiven, the music of being called "blessed" and "beloved," the beauty of holiness, they will experience these wonders in the people of God. Jacob says to his brother Esau, "To see your face is like seeing the face of God—since you have received me with such favor" (Gen. 33:10). We have the privilege of showing God to one another.

The Magi come asking, "Where is the One born to be the Savior?" (AP). People all around us are asking that question. Day in and day out, whether they or we realize it, people express in countless ways the yearning to know and be known by God. We have the privilege of helping them to come to know that God is real, that evil will not have the last word, that even a world where innocents are killed can be transformed if we will allow ourselves to be transformed.

The wonder of God's coming is this: God doesn't want to be our business partner, to relate to us as a favored relative, to live near us or even with us. God wants to live in us and through us. As Matthew 5:14 tells us, we are the light of the world. We are meant to be God's embodied love. When we obey the claims of Christ, we are God's continuing incarnation. Embracing one person at a time, we help those we meet to believe that they matter and that they are embraced by God.

REFLECTION PAGES

DAY 1 REFLECTION

Read Matthew 2:1-18.

Reflect.

The Magi were "overwhelmed with joy" when they found Jesus. Did you feel overwhelmed by joy at any time during Advent? What brought you the greatest joy this holiday season? How has God been part of what brought you joy?

Suppose you had a treasure chest such as the one the Magi may have carried, in which you kept what is most precious to you. Visualize the chest or draw it here. What would be in it?

Twice in this story, God uses dreams to warn people. What dreams can you remember lately? Have you ever received guidance from your dreams? If so, what kind?

Where in the world are parents weeping for their children today? What causes their grief?

Rest.

Hold before God the grieving mothers and fathers of the world. Pray for resolution of whatever problems or conflicts harm children today.

Pray a breath prayer.

For a breath prayer until your next time of reflection, consider praying, "God of love, comfort those in need."

DAY 2 REFLECTION

Read John 10:7-10.

Reflect.

Jesus says that he guides his sheep to "find pasture." What feeds you as a follower of Christ? What spiritual practices and church activities energize you and help you to grow?

_____

_____

_____

_____

_____

_____

What thieves such as worry, fear, insecurity about yourself or your job, or troubled relationships keep you from living the abundant life God wants for you? What might Jesus say to you about the things that hold you back?

_____

_____

_____

_____

_____

_____

Jesus said that he came to give us life abundant. What would a person living life abundantly look like? How would such a person spend time and money? Is this the way you spend your time and money?

What thieves of abundant life exist in your community? What problems such as poverty, racism, classism, lack of education or jobs, or pollution limit life for you and your neighbors? What do you think God wants for you and for your community?

_____

_____

_____

_____

_____

_____

_____

_____

_____

_____

_____

_____

Rest.

Sit in God's presence and ask God to show you what limits you in experiencing fullness of life. Ask God to help you let go of anything that limits you and others.

Pray a breath prayer.

For a breath prayer until your next time of reflection, consider praying, "God of life, help me live fully."

105

DAY 3 REFLECTION

Read Psalm 40:1-10.

Reflect.

Verses 1-3 of this psalm describe the process of God's delivering someone by degrees—out of a pit to a bog to solid rock to singing. Think back to a time when you needed significant change in your life. By what steps did God bring about change?

_____

_____

_____

_____

_____

_____

_____

_____

Imagine being stuck in a pit that you could not climb out of on your own. Have you ever been in a similar situation? How did God help you? Whom did God send to help you?

_____

_____

_____

_____

_____

_____

In what ways do you think people who are addicted are stuck in a pit from which escape is difficult? Who do you know who struggles with addiction? What resources are available in your community to help people with addictions?

_____

_____

_____

_____

_____

_____

In what ways do you praise God for the "deliverance" that you have experienced in your life? How is your faith evident to those who know you? If you think it is not evident, why not?

_____

_____

_____

_____

_____

_____

Rest.

Think about the positive changes in your life over the last five years. How was God active in bringing about those changes? How did God support you in making changes?

Pray a breath prayer.

For a breath prayer until your next time of reflection, consider praying, "Dear God, thank you for freedom."

DAY 4 REFLECTION

Read Revelation 21:1-5 and 22:1-5.

Reflect.

What do you want to see in the "New Jerusalem," the world God is creating?

_____

_____

_____

_____

What do you feel sure will not exist in that new world?

_____

_____

What in your life needs to be "made new"? What needs to be made new in your community? in your country? in the world?

Below or on a separate sheet, draw your concept of a "tree of life" and label it to show what makes a good life. From what ground does a good life grow? What is the strength of a good life? Label the leaves and branches to show what feeds a good life.

Do you know someone experiencing a time of darkness? How can you share God's light in a way that will be meaningful and helpful to that person?

_____

_____

_____

_____

_____

_____

_____

_____

_____

_____

_____

_____

_____

_____

_____

Rest.

Envision life flowing from God into your body, beginning at the top of your head, flowing into your chest, your arms and hands, your torso, your legs and feet. Let the light of God penetrate every part of you. Rest in the light, allowing God to heal you and fill you with joy.

Pray a breath prayer.

For a breath prayer until your next time of reflection, consider praying, "God of light, shine through me."

DAY 5 REFLECTION

Read Isaiah 11:1-9.

Reflect.

What our eyes see and what our ears hear can make hanging on to a vision of peace tough to do. What problems do you see that trouble you, that you want God to solve?

_____

_____

_____

_____

_____

_____

_____

"They will not hurt or destroy," says Isaiah's vision. What changes would cause people to stop hurting and destroying one another and the world? What needs to change within you?

_____

_____

_____

_____

_____

_____

How has knowing God made a difference in you? How has God brought about reconciliation in your life?

_____

_____

_____

_____

In what areas of your life or inner self do you still need to experience peace and reconciliation?

_____

_____

_____

Rest.

Think about a world where the lion can lie down with the lamb, where every child is safe, where peace reigns in every heart. Enjoy the scene. Ask God how you can help to bring that world to reality.

Pray a breath prayer.

For a breath prayer today, consider praying, "God of peace, bring peace through me."

Group Session Plans

These weekly sessions are designed to last about forty-five minutes. Assign a period of time to each section of the session based on the size and personality of your group. Since adults learn best when they have a personal stake in the subject matter and can link it to their lives, each session will invite group members to respond to questions or participate in activities. These questions and activities will help participants in making that connection.

Before You Begin: If your group will meet on a day other than Sunday, schedule your first meeting in the week before the first Sunday in Advent. Your advance publicity should clearly state the schedule. Group members need to read the chapter for each week in advance, so offer copies of the book to participants at least a week before the first session. People can read each chapter of the book in about fifteen minutes; the time needed for daily reflection questions and journaling will of course vary according to the individual. Encourage group members to answer the reflection questions by writing in the book or in a journal, but communicate in the opening session that these responses will always remain private unless individuals choose to discuss them. Have copies of this book available at the first session for those who were unable to get their books in advance. You will need to decide whether to buy "loaner" copies (and how many) to have available for use by visitors and by those who forget to bring their copies to the meetings.

Preparation: The design does not call for extensive leader preparation beyond reading the chapter and doing the daily reflections, though some sessions require the leader to gather materials in advance. A supply list is included at the beginning of each session plan. Leadership may rotate among class or group members. Leaders should contact people in advance to read a scripture passage in the group, participate in a "drama," or pray aloud in class. Some people who would decline or be uncomfortable if asked on the spur of the moment are quite willing to take part if contacted ahead of time.

Each session includes a Christmas carol, so leaders may recruit persons to lead the singing or to at least get the carol started if music is not among the session leader's talents. Provide photocopies of the words for the carols if hymnals or songbooks are not available. Be sure to allow time in each session for the period of silent reflection. Leaders may be tempted to skip this portion more than any other, but silence is important and rare during busy times like Advent. Please make time for this silence rather than rushing to end the meeting by eliminating this portion.

Session 1 calls for viewing a videotape of Christmas commercials taped from television, so ask someone in the group to tape those before the first session. Choose commercials that tell stories—those that set up "people situations" and use actors who do not appear to be salespeople. Choose five or six commercials, thirty to sixty seconds in length. Session 5 (in early January) calls for presenting candles to the participants; you may want to rescue and recycle candles from Christmas Eve candlelight services, if your congregation or community has such services. However, offering small votives in assorted colors can also emphasize that we are different in the ways we share God's light with the world.

Advent Wreath and Christ Candle: At the beginning of each session, light a candle or candles to symbolize Christ's presence with your group. You may want to bring in a small table or a stool draped with a cloth to create a place for the candle(s) each week. An Advent wreath consists of a ring of greenery with four purple candles (or sometimes three purple candles and one rose-colored candle) arranged around its circumference and a single white Christ candle placed in the center of the ring. You may also use a single white pillar candle as a Christ candle each week, without a wreath and additional candles.

To use an Advent wreath, light one additional candle each week in Advent. The first week in Advent, light one purple candle during a litany or while a prayer is read. The second week, light two purple candles during the reading. The third week, light three candles. (If the wreath includes a rose candle, this is the week to light it, along with two purple candles.) The fourth week of Advent, light all four colored candles. On Christmas Eve or Christmas Day, light the Christ candle in the center of the wreath in addition to the purple/rose candles.

Session Components
Lighting of Advent Wreath/Christ Candle
Singing a Christmas Carol
Connecting
Reviewing the Week

Exploring Scripture
Reflecting Silently
Closing: Prayer and sending forth

Supplies: For each session—Advent wreath or Christ candle; wooden matches; photocopies of litany or prayer for the week; the suggested Christmas carol; Bibles or photocopies of scripture verses used in the session; easel with newsprint (or chalkboard/whiteboard) and markers; plain, white index cards (without lines on either side); scissors, colored pens or markers, tape, and glue; ribbon or ornament hooks to use in attaching paper ornaments to your group's Christmas tree; a small Christmas tree that can remain in your meeting place throughout the series. This "tree" could be as simple as a green outline on a piece of poster board set on an easel or mounted on a wall; or it could be a small artificial tree in a base. Each week, the class will add "ornaments" that they create from index cards.

————

SESSION I

LIVING IN HOPE: WHAT WILL YOU GIVE ME?

Special preparation for leader: Read Genesis 38; Joshua 2; and Joshua 6:22-25 in order to be able to guide the retelling of the stories in the Exploring Scripture section.

Additional supplies for this session:
- photocopies of the explanation of the breath prayer from page 11
- a VCR, monitor or television, and videotape of assorted Christmas television commercials being seen in your area OR color Christmas ads torn from magazines, enough for each person in the group to have an ad. Test the video equipment before class begins and cue the tape to begin, in order to minimize class time spent wrestling with technology.
- photocopies of Joshua 2 and Joshua 6:22-25
- "O Come, All Ye Faithful"

Lighting of Advent Wreath
Singing a Christmas Carol: "O Come, All Ye Faithful"
Introducing the Study

This introduction plus the "connecting" section will take more time in this meeting than in later sessions.

Step 1: Introduce participants to the series. Ask whether folks obtained their copies of the book and were able to begin with the readings and reflection. (Have additional copies of the book available for those who were not able to get their copies in advance.) The object is not to see if they've "done their homework" but to be sure participants understand what you will be doing each week during sessions and between them. Explain to participants that there is a short chapter to read each week, along with daily reflections for five days (not six or seven).

Step 2: Reassure participants that their responses to the reflection questions will remain private unless they choose to talk about what they wrote. Mention that the questions may be answered by writing either in the book or in a separate notebook or journal. Stress that the questions are meant to spark reflection and do not have right and wrong answers. Since some participants probably will not be familiar with journaling, ask for a show of hands of those who have experience with journaling or with writing responses to reflection questions for a small-group study. Then ask for volunteers among those who raised their hands to say how that experience worked and what they got out of it. Though writing is difficult for some, encourage people to try the process and not to be too harsh with themselves if they can't do it every day. Advent is a busy time, and any writing they are able to do can be productive in guiding them to new insights.

Step 3: Distribute a photocopy of the section from the Introduction that explains the breath prayer to those who do not have their books with them. Ask if anyone in the group has practiced this way of praying. If so and if the person(s) is/are willing, invite each one to talk about this way of praying. If no one in the group has tried the breath prayer or no one can talk about it, allow time for everyone to read the page. Then lead the group in praying the shortened form of the prayer ("Lord Jesus Christ, have mercy").

Outline the following steps for the group: Before beginning the breath prayer, you will say the words aloud several times and then be quiet, allowing people to continue praying the prayer on their own. You will end the prayer time by saying "amen," after allowing them to pray the prayer silently for a while.

Instruct group members to adjust their sitting position until they are comfortable, with their shoulders, arms, and hands relaxed. Tell them to take several deep breaths. Then invite them to pray silently as you pray aloud, matching the rhythm of their breathing to the words. Pray the prayer quietly and slowly, repeating the words five or six times. Allow about one minute of silence before saying "amen."

Remind participants that although the reflection pages suggest new, short breath prayers throughout Advent, they can create their own breath prayer at any time or continue praying any of the suggested breath prayers for as long as they wish.

Connecting

Step 1: *(Using videotape will be the least time-consuming way to do this step.)* Remind the class that this first week of Advent focuses on hope, then introduce the videotape of Christmas commercials. Before showing the videotape, instruct participants to ask themselves this question as they watch the commercials: What are people in the ads hoping for? Suggest that the products in the ads and what the ads are "selling" may differ. For instance, ads for toothpaste (the product) may actually be selling sex appeal and acceptance; ads for fast cars (cars are the product) may actually be selling an image of success. View the commercials.

ALTERNATIVE **Step 1:** If you do not have the means to tape and view commercials, make the point about the difference between products in ads and what ads are selling, then direct group members to search magazines for Christmas ads. Do the exercise with these print ads.

A third alternative (the least effective one) is requesting folks to describe popular commercials they have seen or have heard people talk about this holiday season. List on the board or newsprint short descriptive phrases so class members can remember the commercials.

Step 2: After reviewing the ads, ask, "What hopes do you see pictured and implied in these ads?" Using the chalkboard or newsprint, mark off three columns, titling the first one "Ads." In this column, list the hopes people name.

Step 3: Ask, "How does this list compare to the hope of Christmas that we talk about in church?" Title the second column "Church" and list these responses in the second column.

Reviewing the Week

Step 1: Ask, "How do these images compare to the comments about hope found in the reading and reflections this week?" Title the third column "Reading" and list phrases from the responses.

Step 2: Direct participants to form small groups of two or three people. Ask the small groups to discuss one of these two sets of questions: Allow participants two minutes per person to respond.

"Did you highlight or underline passages in the reading? If so, what was it about the passages that caused you to do so?"

Or, "Which day's reflection did you find most meaningful or challenging? Why?"

Step 3: Still addressing the small groups, ask, "How do these lists compare with the hopes you personally have for this Christmas season?" Allow two minutes per person for response. Then invite group members to mention their hopes to the larger group.

Exploring Scripture

Distribute photocopies of the Bible passages so participants will have them in hand for the next part of the discussion.

Telling the Bible stories. Invite session participants to retell the Bible story of Tamar and Judah by saying one sentence each. Ask for a volunteer to start the story. Then explain to everyone how to link each succeeding sentence to the one before by saying, "And then" or "But before that" or "And while that was happening." (You may want to write these phrases on the board or newsprint as a reminder.) For instance, one person might begin by saying, "Er, Tamar's husband, dies because he was wicked." The next person might say, "But before that, Judah got Tamar as a bride for him," or another might continue, "And then Judah tells his next son, Onan, to take Tamar as his wife," or another might say, "And while that was happening, Tamar continues waiting and waiting and waiting."

Have the group members retell the story of Rahab using the same format.

Ask the participants, "Why do you think the Bible mentions these women in Jesus' genealogy? What makes their stories important to us?" Allow participants to respond.

Then ask, "How do these stories illustrate hope?"

Expressing insights. Distribute the index cards, colored pens or markers, and scissors. Invite class members to draw a symbol on the index card or write a word that represents something from the Bible passage or the discussion that represents hope. Then have people cut out what they have drawn or written, decorate the disk, and attach it to the tree using ribbon, tape, ornament hooks, or paper clips.

Reflecting Silently

Invite participants to become still and to listen as you guide them in thinking about a passage of scripture. Read Habakkuk 2:1-4 slowly. Then ask the following questions, pausing for thirty seconds before moving to the next question. Use a watch with a second hand to be sure you allow the full time for quiet reflection.

Say, "Picture Habakkuk standing guard on the ramparts. He might say, as the psalmist did, 'I wait for the LORD, . . . more than those who watch for the morning.'" Ask: "What are you guarding this Advent? What has God given you to take care of?"

Repeat the phrase from Psalm 130 again: "I wait for the LORD, . . . more than those who watch for the morning." Ask: "What are you waiting for and watching for? What image on the horizon would delight you?"

Closing

Prayer. God of hope, we come to you with our questions and with our hopes, grateful that you welcome us just as we are. We name silently in our hearts our desires for the coming days . . . *[pause to allow time for thought and prayer].* Increase our attentiveness to you during the coming week, that we may see signs of your working all around us. Show us how to wait with you in hope. Amen.

Sending forth. Say, "Hear this benediction from Romans 15: 'May the God of hope fill you with all joy and peace in believing.'"

Extinguish the candle and say, "Go in peace and in hope."

SESSION 2

FINDING A HOME: WHY HAVE I FOUND FAVOR IN YOUR SIGHT?

Special preparation for leader: (1) In advance, ask five persons to be prepared to read parts of the story of Ruth from the Bible. One person will be a narrator; the other four will be Ruth, Naomi, Boaz, and the unnamed kinsman. The readers may want to read the story ahead of time. (2) Photocopy the necessary pages for each person and mark each page for the speaker by bracketing or highlighting all that speaker's passages. For example, mark all the narrator's speeches on one copy, all of Naomi's speeches on another, and so on. Give these to the readers at the beginning of the group meeting. (3) Read the "Exploring Scripture" meditation until you are comfortable with leading the group through it. Practice pausing and judge how long pauses should be by reflecting on the questions yourself until you have a sense of how long people will need to follow the direction.

> *Additional supplies for this session:*
> - photocopies of scripture reading
> - "O Come, O Come, Emmanuel"
> - Christmas music and a tape or CD player for a game of musical chairs and a piece of Christmas candy as a prize for the winner

Lighting of Advent Wreath/Christ Candle
Singing a Christmas Carol: "O Come, O Come, Emmanuel"
Connecting

Step 1: The theme of this week is preparation. Begin by asking, "How many of you are ready for Christmas?" After the groans and laughter subside, remind the group of the theme for this week. Draw a vertical line on the board or easel, dividing the space into two columns. At the top of the left column, write "Preparing Yourself." At the top of the right column, write "Preparing the Church." Ask what people are doing to prepare themselves and what preparations they observe in the church. Complete the lists one at a time.

Step 2: After developing the lists, ask the group to look at them. Note how many items on the list concern preparation of their homes, how many concern preparation that will benefit others (such as buying gifts, addressing Christmas cards), and how many concern preparation that actually is individual and personal—for them alone. (You can indicate the individual items by starring, circling, underlining in another color, placing an initial alongside, or marking them by some other means.) Ask the group to comment on what they think the lists reveal.

Step 3: Someone probably will note that participating in the study group is part of their preparation, but if not, point out that reading books about Advent and participating in study groups are ways we prepare ourselves.

Step 4: Read aloud Isaiah 40:3-5. Ask, "What are the bumps in the road and the obstacles, the things that need to be cleared, in order for us to welcome Christ this Christmas? What stands in the way of our experiencing these days of Advent as spiritual time?"

Reviewing the Week

Breath prayers. Ask, "What was your experience with the breath prayers this week?" Model for the group by reporting whether you practiced this way of praying or were too busy. Comment whether it did or didn't "work" for you if you tried it. Someone may suggest composing a common breath prayer for all the participants in the group to pray as a group discipline during Advent, rather than praying different breath prayers every day.

Reflection and journaling. Let the group form into triads. Invite them talk in these smaller groups about the reading and daily exercises for the week. First question: "What do you remember from the reading?" Allow one minute for each person to respond. Second question: "Which daily reflection did you find most challenging or most interesting? Why?" Allow two minutes per person for responses.

Exploring Scripture

Step 1: Ask for volunteers to play a game of musical chairs, or, if the group is small, invite everyone to participate. To play: Assemble chairs in a circle or back to back, one fewer chairs than persons playing, so that someone will be without a chair. Players stand and walk around the chairs while the music plays. When the music stops, everyone tries to find a seat. Someone will be left out. Have that person stop playing. Remove one chair and start the music again, repeating the process until only one person remains. Give the winner a piece of Christmas candy as a prize. Ask the group, "What does this game show us about being an outsider and not having a place?"

Step 2: After their responses, invite the readers to "perform" the story of Ruth while the other group members listen, thinking of the characters as "outsiders" in their settings.

NARRATOR: Ruth 1:1-8
NAOMI: Ruth 1:8*b*
NARRATOR: Ruth 1:14
RUTH: Ruth 1:16-17
NARRATOR: Ruth 1:19
NAOMI: Ruth 1:20-21
NARRATOR: And so Ruth went to glean in the fields of Elimelech's kinsman Boaz. Boaz heard about the young foreigner who worked hard and honored her mother-in-law. Boaz told his workers to leave extra grain for Ruth to pick up and to be sure that no one bothered her. But Naomi wanted more for Ruth than being a gleaner. She wanted Ruth to have security and respect.
NAOMI: Ruth 3:1-4
RUTH: Ruth 3:5*b*
NARRATOR: Ruth 3:7-8
BOAZ: Who are you?
RUTH: "I am Ruth, your handmaid. . . ."
BOAZ: Ruth 3:10-13
NARRATOR: In the morning Boaz said: "Bring the cloak you are wearing and hold it out." And he measured out six measures of barley. Ruth took a gift from Boaz to her mother-in-law, Naomi, who said,
NAOMI: Ruth 3:18
NARRATOR: So Boaz waited at the city gate until the nearer kinsman came by. Boaz said to him,
BOAZ: Ruth 4:3-4
KINSMAN: I will redeem it.
BOAZ: Ruth 4:5
KINSMAN: Ruth 4:6
NARRATOR: Ruth 4:13-16

Step 3: Invite members of the group to be silent. Explain that the group is going to reflect silently on the story and that you will be making suggestions and asking questions to guide them in this meditation on the scripture. Speak slowly and clearly, pausing when that seems natural, even if a pause is not indicated in the text. Tell people to make themselves comfortable and to relax. Encourage people to allow whatever happens for them during the meditation to happen. If they fall asleep or their minds wander, that is fine.

Say, "You may want to close your eyes as you listen, to help you concentrate. Now, use your imagination to identify with the story at the moment Naomi and Ruth say good-bye to Orpah. Let yourself be in the scene with them. *[Pause]* What do you see? Who else is there? *[Pause]* What emotions do you see in their faces? Curiosity? Disinterest? Sadness? Disapproval? *[Pause]* Look at Naomi's face. What feelings do you see there? What do you sense from her?

"Imagine that you have known these women for several years. What makes Naomi able to set out for Bethlehem? What experiences made her a woman who could return to Bethlehem?

"Let yourself see Ruth. What emotions do you sense in her? What makes Ruth able to leave Moab? What experiences made her this kind of young woman?

"Let yourself see Orpah as she turns to go home to her father's house. Is she crying? Is she concerned about Naomi and Ruth? *[Pause]* Has Orpah always been less than adventurous, so that you knew she would stay in Moab? Or are you surprised that she chooses not to go along with the other two women? *[Pause]* What experiences have made her the kind of person who stays?

"In your imagination, see the women leaving. Watch Orpah go into her family home. Watch Ruth and Naomi move away into the distance. *[Pause]* Let the images fade in your mind, and come back to our meeting in this room."

Step 4: Ask the group, "What came to mind about these women? What sorts of experiences did you imagine might have led them to do what they did?" After people share their responses and speculations, go on to step 5.

Step 5: Say the following or paraphrase it in a form comfortable for you: "We cannot know what experiences formed the people in this story, what made them able to risk or unable to risk. But we know that God used the circumstances and experiences of Naomi, Ruth, and Boaz's lives to prepare them for a role in the coming of the Messiah. That knowledge suggests thinking about 'preparing for Christmas' in another way. We prepare our hearts to welcome Christ, but God also works to prepare us. How has God been preparing us and the world to welcome Christ this Christmas?"

Invite participants to respond. At some point in the discussion, state explicitly that God did not want Naomi's husband and sons to die. God does not send tragedy into our lives to build character or to bring us to acknowledge our need for Christ. God wills "life, and that . . . abundantly" (John 10:10, KJV) for us. But all the experiences of our lives mold us, and God works through our personality and experiences.

Expressing insights. Hand out the index cards, pens or markers, and scissors. Invite participants to draw a symbol or write a word on the card to represent the idea of preparing. Everyone may decorate their ornaments and add them to the Christmas tree.

Reflecting Silently

Invite everyone to become silent again. Say, "Deuteronomy 8:2 states, 'Remember the long way that the LORD your God has led you.' Looking back over your life, identify two or three choices you made that changed your direction. *[Pause to allow time for reflection.]* Can you see in retrospect that God used those choices to bring you where you are today? *[Pause]* How has God prepared you and brought you into this group for this Advent?" *[Allow time for reflection.]*

Closing

Prayer. God of many roads, we give thanks that you have brought each of us here today by way of our widely differing paths. We give thanks that you took notice of us and that you invite us to become part of the family. Help us to see any obstacles that stand in the way of our welcoming you this Advent, to do what we can to remove them, and to know that you are constantly clearing the way for us to embrace you. In the name of Jesus, the Christ, we pray.

Sending forth. Say, "Hear this benediction drawn from Philippians 1:6: Go in confidence of this: God who has begun a good work in you will continue it until the day of Jesus Christ."

Extinguish the candle and say, "Go in peace."

SESSION 3

THE WONDER OF BEING SOUGHT:

WHY HAS THIS HAPPENED TO ME?

Special preparation for leader: Create message cards for each person in the group. (You may need extras for visitors.) Each card should read as follows:

> *[Blank for name],*
> Blessed are you, for God delights in you.
> I give thanks that God is blessing the world through you.

If you have access to a computer and printer, you may print the words on adhesive labels, then place the labels on index cards. Or you may type or print the message on the cards.

Additional supplies for this session:
- photocopies of Luke 1:24-25, 39-45
- "Joy to the World"
- assorted note cards or note paper, envelopes, and pens

Lighting of Advent Wreath
Singing a Christmas Carol: "Joy to the World"
Connecting
    Step 1: The theme for this week is joy. Begin by asking group members to think about the happiest day of their life—so far. Give them time to sort through their memories and choose the day. Then ask them to go, in their minds, to that time and place. Give them a few moments. Then say, "You don't have to say what the occasion was, but consider what it was about the situation that made you feel so happy. What word would you use?" If responses are very slow to come, suggest some words such as *accomplishment, beauty, fulfillment, people, freedom, recognition.* After listening to the responses, remind the group that the theme for this week of Advent is joy. **Note:** Some people debate the difference between *joy* and *happiness,* but for our purposes either word can denote a feeling of gladness. It is not necessary to attribute a "religious" connotation to either word.

Step 2: Although the media and the culture communicate that the Christmas season is supposed to be a joyful time of year, some people find this season difficult because they do not feel happy or joyful. It is important to acknowledge this reality. Ask the group, "What contributes to feeling joyful at this time, and what interferes with feeling joyful?" List their responses.

Step 3: Remind the group that cultural celebration of the season often neglects the religious significance of Christmas. Ask the group, "What is the difference between the happiness we see portrayed in Christmas movies and the happiness or joy that Christian believers can find in this season?"

Reviewing the Week

Step 1: By now this step should be familiar to the group. Ask the members to form triads and answer the questions.

"Did you highlight or underline passages in the reading? If so, what was it about the passages that prompted you to underline them?" (Allow two minutes per person for responses.)

"Which day's reflection did you find most meaningful or challenging? Why?" (Allow two minutes per person for responses.)

Step 2: While participants are still in small groups, ask them to respond to this question: "Think about your image of the happiest day in your life—so far. What can you do or are you doing to experience that joy during this Advent season?"

Exploring Scripture

Step 1: Distribute the copies of the passage from Luke 1. Ask group members to read one verse each in turn. Ask, "Why do you think Elizabeth's words to Mary were important enough to be included in the Bible?" (Allow one minute per person for responses in the small groups.)

Step 2: Then ask, "Who has been like Elizabeth in your life? Who has helped you, through either words or actions, to know yourself as 'blessed'?" (Allow two minutes per person for responses in the small groups.)

Step 3: Finally, ask, "Who has helped you to be aware of God's working in your life? Who or what has helped you to see yourself as someone through whom God can bless the world? Or is it hard for you to see yourself that way?"

Step 4: Tell the group members that you are going to experience blessing one another. Invite people to put down anything they may be holding and to relax. Ask them to listen as you read some scripture passages. Read the following passages.

"So God created humankind in his image, in the image of God . . . God blessed them, and . . . God saw everything that he had made, and indeed it was very good" (Gen. 1:27, 28, 31).

"The LORD God says, 'Here is my servant, whom I uphold, my chosen, in whom my soul delights; I have put my spirit upon him; . . . I am the Lord, I have called you in righteousness, I have taken you by the hand and will keep you; I have given you as a covenant to the people, a light to the Gentiles" (Isa. 42:1, 6).

Then say, "God pronounces each of us 'blessed' and blesses the world through us. We have the privilege and responsibility to help one another believe and experience that blessing. I invite you within your groups to bless one another in turn. We will do this by making the sign of the cross in the palm of the hand, making eye contact, and saying the person's name, followed by, 'Blessed are you, for God delights in you. I give thanks that God comes into the world through you.'" Distribute cards with the blessing and blank for the recipient's name.

Decide who will say the first blessing, then explain, "Each of us will bless the person to our right. To begin, the person to the right of [name of person who will start] will extend a hand, palm upward. In turn, the person blessing traces the sign of the cross with his or her finger in the other's upturned palm [demonstrate by tracing a cross on your own palm] and pronounces the blessing. Now, before we bless one another, let us quiet ourselves and pray."

Pray this prayer: "O God, your love overwhelms us. It is more than we can comprehend. We give thanks that you claim each of us and name us blessed. Help us to express this truth in our words and in our deeds. Amen. Let us bless one another." (Allow two minutes for people to pass the blessing.)

Step 5: Distribute the pens. Ask participants to write on the blessing card the name of the person they blessed and to give that person the card. Direct group members to take their cards home and put them in a place where it will remind them that they are wonderful.

Expressing insights. Hand out the supplies for making ornaments and invite each group member to create another ornament for the tree, one that symbolizes joy and being blessed.

Reflecting Silently

Say to the participants, "Each of us has the power to bless others by our words, and people long for words of affirmation. Think about two people you see in your day-to-day activities, especially those you see daily or almost daily. *[Pause]* Consider them one by one. What gifts does the first one bring to your life? *[Pause]* What gifts does the second one bring to your life? *[Pause]* Give thanks for the role these individuals play in your life."

Distribute the note cards, envelopes, and pens. Say, "Take time right now to write a few sentences of appreciation to one of these persons. It does not have to be elaborate or eloquent. You may say something like, 'Thank you for being patient with me and helping me day after day,' or, 'Your cheerfulness makes a difference in my days. Thanks.' Take an extra note card or two with you if you'd like, and later today write a note to other people you thought of."

Closing

Prayer. God of love, we bless you and give thanks that you pronounce each one of us blessed, precious, and honored. Go with us through this week and empower us to bless each person we meet. May our words and actions convey your love. We pray this in the name of Jesus. Amen.

Sending forth. Say, "Hear this benediction drawn from Isaiah 43:1 and 43:4: 'God says to you, 'I have called you by name; you are mine. You are precious in my sight, and honored, and I love you.'"

Or read this passage from Numbers 6:24:

The LORD bless you and keep you;
the LORD make his face to shine upon you,
and be gracious to you;
the LORD lift up his countenance upon you and give you peace.

Extinguish the candle and say, "Go in peace and joy."

SESSION 4

WRESTLING WITH MYSTERY: HOW CAN THIS BE?

Special preparation for leader: Recruit in advance two extroverted people from the class, or if your church has a drama group, ask two of those performers to role play the angel Gabriel's visit to Mary.

In the role play, Mary's attitude should not be portrayed as sweet and submissive. Mary is rational and needs to be convinced, first that Gabriel really is an angel and then that he has gotten the message right. Mary suggests alternative messages and then, grasping the incredible content of the actual message, suggests alternative young women for the task. Gabriel is weary, having already visited several other young women with the same message and been turned down flat.

Encourage the players to use contemporary language and to "ham it up," to behave as if the event were happening today. They may refer to science-fiction movies and characters and to Old Testament miracles in talking about what Mary is willing or not willing to believe, sort of ranking miracles in believability. Mary may be dressed as a teenager, though not too outrageous a teenager. Gabriel needs only a halo made from a coat hanger and headband and some paper wings pinned to his or her shoulders.

Additional supplies for this session:
- photocopies of Luke 1:26-38
- "What Child Is This?" or "My Soul Gives Glory to My God"
- small strips of paper or note cards and pens
- a gift-wrapped box big enough to hold the strips of paper or note cards (Wrap the top and bottom of the box separately so the top can be removed during the session and the strips of paper or note cards placed inside.)

Lighting of Advent Wreath
Singing a Christmas Carol: "My Soul Gives Glory to My God"
Connecting

Step 1: Remind the group of the week's theme: the mystery of the Incarnation. Mention that the scripture includes the angel's visit to Mary and Mary's responses.

Step 2: Ask the group, "How does God get your attention? How does God 'speak' to you?" List on newsprint or the board the ways people mention.

Step 3: Ask, "How do you think a visit from an angel would be better than the ways we've listed?" Record their responses.

Step 4: Ask, "How do you think a visit from an angel would be worse than these ways?" Record their responses.

Step 5: Ask, "What would you need to convince you to obey God in doing something that might result in your being censured by the community and disgraced? Is it possible to convince someone about matters of faith?" Allow participants to discuss their answers.

Say, "Today we'll discuss the questions we bring to God about Christmas and about other things."

Reviewing the Week

Have the group form triads. Ask the following questions and let people respond in their small groups.

"Are you able to pray the breath prayers? How do you feel about the practice after this length of time?"

"Did you highlight or underline passages in the reading this week? If so, describe what caught your attention in these passages." (Allow two minutes per person for responses.)

"Which day's reflection did you find most meaningful or challenging? Why?" (Allow two minutes per person for responses.)

Exploring Scripture

Invite the players to perform the scene of Gabriel's visit to Mary (three to five minutes). After the performance, ask the group, "What new perspectives did this portrayal of the angel's visit give you about the Annunciation and Mary?" If the following ideas do not come out in the group discussion, point out

- that Mary's question did not disqualify her from participating in the events of Christmas;
- that Gabriel stayed with Mary until she was able to accept what God was asking her to do;
- that questions about God and what God asks of us can be explored without negative consequences.

128

Expressing insights. Hand out the supplies for making ornaments and invite each group member to create another ornament for the tree, this time one that symbolizes questions.

Reflecting Silently

Step 1: Say, "I am going to read some verses about Thomas, whom we often call Doubting Thomas. Though doubts and questions are not exactly the same, the way Christ dealt with Thomas's doubts gives us an idea of how God responds to us when we have questions related to our faith. As I read, imagine the scene described in this passage from the Gospel of John."

Step 2: Read John 20:24-29 slowly and reflectively. Then say, "I am going to lead you through parts of the scripture again." Reread John 20:25 and say, "In silence, think about Thomas when he expressed his doubts. What do you suppose he was feeling?" *[Pause]*

Reread John 20:27 and say, "Now think about Jesus approaching Thomas. Let yourself imagine the love and concern on Jesus' face as he steps closer to Thomas and extends his hands. *[Pause]* Picture Jesus extending his hands to Thomas, inviting Thomas to touch the wounds. *[Pause]* Imagine Thomas responding. Does he reach out eagerly? slowly? not at all? *[Pause]* Let yourself see Thomas's face as awareness dawns. What do you see in Thomas's face as he says, 'My Lord and my God!'?" *[Pause]*

Step 3: Say, "Now I invite you to think about yourself. What questions sometimes keep you from being involved in what God is doing? *[Pause]* Let yourself see Christ gazing at you in understanding and love. *[Pause]* Are you willing to leave your questions with God this Christmas and accept mystery?"

Step 4: Distribute the paper or cards and pens and say, "I invite you to write down on these pieces of paper [or, these cards] the questions you sometimes struggle with, on your own behalf or for others. No one will see what you write. Then I will pass this box around [the gift-wrapped one]. Place your questions in the box as a sign of your willingness to live with mystery and unanswered questions, and we will make this our gift to God."

Step 5: Allow time for participants to write, then pass the box (with the lid in place, so that anything written on the paper/cards remains private).

Step 6: Place the box containing the participants' notes under the tree. Then invite the class to join you in the closing prayer.

Closing

Prayer. God of Mystery, we acknowledge that we cannot know you fully or comprehend all that you do. But we believe that you are a God of love, and so we entrust our questions to your love. Help us in this Advent season to experience your reality in new ways. Amen.

Sending forth. Say, "Hear this benediction drawn from John 20 and Hebrews 13:5: Go in the company of Christ who drew near to Thomas in his doubting, Christ who has promised never to forsake us."

Extinguish the candle and say, "Go in peace."

———

SESSION 5

SHARING THE LIGHT: WHERE IS THE CHILD?

Additional supplies for this session:

- Photocopies of the Bible passage Matthew 2:1-23
- "We Three Kings" or, if available, "Some Children See Him"
- Copies of the Sunday newspaper or the collected daily newspapers for the week, enough for each person to have a section
- Copies of your church's budget, one for each person
- One candle for each group member (These could be the tiny candles used on birthday cakes, or you may be able to rescue and recycle candles from a candle-light service if your church or community has one. Or you may want to bring an assortment of small votive candles in varied colors, sizes, and scents, to represent the diversity of people in the group.)

Lighting of Advent Wreath
Singing a Christmas Carol: "We Three Kings" (or "Some Children See Him")
Connecting

Step 1: Write on the board or easel the four questions from the session titles with the emphasis word alongside (*hope, preparation, joy, Incarnation*). Review these quickly. You may need to remind folks of the earlier content.

Step 2: Before participants arrive, write this message on the board in large letters:

"Christmas is over. Now we can get back to our real lives and our usual way of doing things."

Step 3: Distribute the newspapers. Direct participants to find two kinds of items: one suggesting that the light of Christ is shining in your community, the nation, or the world; and one suggesting a place or situation in need of Christ's light and love.

Step 4: Ask people to report on the news items about where the light of Christ is shining. Then ask for reports on items about situations in which Christ is needed or is needed more. Note whether each situation is one that an individual could address or one that requires a group's response.

Step 5: Direct attention to the "Christmas is over . . ." message. Ask, "If we return to our usual way of doing things, how will the light of Christ reach these places and situations where it is needed?"

Step 6: Remind the class that the week's theme is the story of the Magi who came seeking Christ. If there are Hispanic participants or those who have lived in Hispanic countries, ask one of them to explain to the group the tradition of Three Kings Day. If no one has this information, explain to the group that some Latin and Spanish countries celebrate Three Kings Day, January 6, rather than December 25 as the day to exchange Christmas gifts. The occasion commemorates the Magi's visit and gifts to the Christ child. Remind people also that Epiphany (January 6) is the real "twelfth day of Christmas," or Christmastide, as counted from the day after Christmas. Point out that this is a clear signal that Christmas is not supposed to be "over" before the new year begins.

Reviewing the Week

Have the group form triads to answer the questions.

"Have you been able to pray a breath prayer? If so, how do you feel about the practice after this length of time?"

"Did you highlight or underline passages in the reading this week? If so, what was it about the passages that caused you to do so?" (Allow two minutes per person for responses.)

"Which day's reflection did you find most meaningful or challenging? Why?" (Allow two minutes per person for responses.)

Exploring Scripture

Step 1: Ask the group, "What do we know about the Magi?" List responses on newsprint or the board.

Step 2: Read Matthew 2:1-18, asking each participant to read a verse in turn. Then ask, "How many of the things on this list are not included in the scripture passage that we just read?" Mark the items on the list that do not come from Matthew's account.

Step 3: Ask, "Why do you think we usually don't read this entire story during Advent? Why do we ignore the slaughter of the children in Bethlehem?"

Step 4: Ask the group to listen for phrases that describe Jesus as you read Luke 2:29-32 aloud. Ask them to mention the phrases and list them on newsprint. Then ask, "How is this picture of Jesus different than our image of the baby in the manger?" Point out that the "real world" is quite willing to welcome a cuddly baby but doesn't like a Savior who shakes things up and causes trouble.

Step 5: Distribute copies of your church's budget. Ask the group members to try to determine your church's priorities by examining the budget. Ask people to name what seems important to your congregation, based on the expenditures the church makes. List the areas named on newsprint or the board.

Step 6: Return to the list of places where Christ is needed in your community or the wider world. Ask participants which of these needs your church is addressing as reflected in the budget's priorities. Explore with the group whether people would like to see any changes in these priorities. If there is interest in trying to meet a need identified from looking at the newspapers, ask the group to identify what steps might be taken to do so.

Reflecting Silently

Say, "Listen to these words from Ephesians 5:8-9: 'Once you were darkness, but now in the Lord you are light. Live as children of light—for the fruit of the light is found in all that is good and right and true.' *[Pause]*

"Where can you take the light of Christ? Which need that we identified does God want you to respond to? What is your personal 'next step'?" *[Pause to give participants time to reflect.]*

Pass the container of candles and invite each participant to take a candle home as a reminder that we are God-bearers, bearing God's light into the world, whenever and wherever we give ourselves over to love.

Closing

Prayer. God who is Love, let your light shine through each of us so that all the world may find its way to you. May your love, compassion, and welcome be incarnate in us, day by day. Amen.

Sending forth. Say, "Hear this benediction drawn from Matthew 5:14 and Ephesians 5:8: Go from here knowing that you are the light of the world. Walk as children of light."

Extinguish the candle and say, "Go in peace."

ABOUT THE AUTHOR

Mary Lou Redding serves as the managing editor of *The Upper Room* daily devotional guide. In addition, she leads retreats and writers' workshops in the U.S. and abroad. Her writings have appeared in numerous magazines, including *Alive Now, Weavings, Christian Writer,* and *Solo.* She is the author of *Breaking and Mending: Divorce and God's Grace* (Upper Room Books, 1998) and a contributor to the *Spiritual Formation Bible* (Zondervan, 1999).

Mary Lou received her Bachelor of Arts degree in English Literature from Oral Roberts University and her Master of Arts in Rhetoric and Writing from the University of Tulsa. She has pursued further study at Vanderbilt University and completed the Academy of Spiritual Formation offered by The Upper Room.

Mary Lou has one adult daughter, loves word games and racquetball, and is a fan of the Atlanta Braves.